Refiner's Fire is a ⎯ ˙ and redemptive power of God! I have known Kay for several years as an ambassador for Moms in Prayer International. She has faithfully served as Regional Coordinator in Swaziland and South Africa for some time, but what I did *not* know is that her life has been a daily adventure of trusting the Lord in the darkest of human circumstances. Her accounts in this book are spiritually riveting, tear inducing, and laugh-out-loud humorous at times. I will never look at a blue box of mac and cheese in the same way! This book is a gift (as is Kay to our Swazi sisters). My life is forever changed by reading "Refiner's Fire."
Cathi Armitage
Global Ministry Director, Moms in Prayer International

I have witnessed John and Kay leave lucrative careers and the comforts of life in the USA to follow the call to Africa. Story after Story in "Refiner's Fire" reveals the sacrifice. Page after page presents riveting, compelling, and poignant narratives of changed lives that would not have been possible without a huge cost. If you want to know more about the privilege of losing your life for His sake, this book is a must.
Doreen Strohm
Co-director, Jesus Cares Ministries

Kay West's book is an honest look at missionary life. Her storytelling holds humor and heart-felt love for the people God brought her to serve. She uses wonderful word pictures to

share the joys and the hardships of life in southern Africa. I highly recommend this book!
Kathryn Coffelt
Global Translation Coordinator, Moms in Prayer International

Refiner's Fire

Refiner's Fire

My Walk with God in the Kingdom of Swaziland

Kay Cassidy West

All scripture taken from the New King James Version of the Holy Bible.

Cover photo credit: Alan Poulson/Shutterstock.com

Copyright © 2016 Kay Cassidy West
All rights reserved.

ISBN-13: 9781539562412
ISBN-10: 1539562417
Library of Congress Control Number: 2016918313
CreateSpace Independent Publishing Platform
North Charleston, South Carolina

*This book is dedicated to the women of Swaziland.
You are my heroes.*

Contents

Acknowledgements · xi
Prelude · xv

1 From Travertine to Linoleum · · · · · · · · · · · · · · · · · · 1
2 No More Chickens in the Car! · · · · · · · · · · · · · · · · ·8
3 Meshach and Abednego, Minus Shadrach · · · · · · · · · 17
4 Stinky Lion Breath · 33
5 From Bad Beer to New Wine · · · · · · · · · · · · · · · · · · 47
6 "Mhlengi is broken! Mhlengi is broken!" · · · · · · · · · · · 61
7 A Teddy Bear's Gift · 74
8 A Supper of Almonds, Mints, and Beef Jerky · · · · · · · 83
9 A Man Named "Wonderful" · · · · · · · · · · · · · · · · · · 95
10 And the Walls Came Tumbling Down · · · · · · · · · · · 109
11 Eighty-Five Boxes of Macaroni and Cheese · · · · · · · · 127
12 "All I know is that I love Jesus and that
   Jesus loves me." · 138
13 Boo Boos and Brushing the Dirt Off · · · · · · · · · · · · 151
14 Joy on a Grass Mat · 162

Postlude: Ncamsile's Story · 171
About the Author · 183

Acknowledgements

I give thanks to my Lord Jesus Christ—for everything.

I thank God for my husband, John West, for walking through the fire with me. We both know there is no way I could have withstood the flames without you. Thank you as well for encouraging, coaching, and loving me through this process.

Thank you to my sons, Zachariah West and Jeremiah West for always encouraging me in the dreams God placed in my heart.

Thank you to Margaret Reis, a friend I have never deserved but for whom I always thank God, for the countless hours you have spent encouraging and editing.

Thank you to Pastor La'Salette Duarte, who welcomed us with open arms to serve alongside her in ministry.

Thank you to our Swaziserve board members, Tom and Doreen Strohm, for being willing to do the arduous work of challenging us, exhorting us, guiding us, and loving us.

Thank you to Pastor Gregg Cantelmo and the Bridgeway Community Church mission team led by Todd Rehn for your steadfast support.

Thank you to Moms in Prayer International, for the profound impact you've had not only on my life, but also on the lives of countless others all over the world.

Thank you to my Swazi interpreters who became so much more: my teachers, my comrades in arms, my friends.

I will bring the one-third through the fire, will refine them as silver is refined, and test them as gold is tested. They will call on My name and I will answer them. I will say, "This is My people," and each one will say, "The LORD is my God." Zechariah 13:9

Prelude

My favorite aroma in the entire world is that of burning sugar cane fields. I came to know this sticky-sweet fragrance as a peculiar gift from God when He saw fit to bless my husband, younger son and me by allowing us to serve Him in the kingdom of Swaziland, where the predominant commodity is sugar. Our family lived and worked in a rural area surrounded by miles and miles and miles of sugar cane. Part of the harvesting process there for sugar is to set fire to several fields a day. I hope I never cease to be amazed and awed by the sight of a field blazing several stories high, a towering inferno that should arouse in even the most callous atheist a healthy fear of hell. For me, it has become a vivid depiction of what our Lord Jesus Christ does for us when we follow in complete surrender to Him. He burns away the chaff and radically changes our hearts for our good and His glory. This is my story of how He has been refining me and the women He has placed in my life. Because it is also God's story, it is beautiful.

Swaziland is a true kingdom, with a king whose rule is absolute. When we were living there, it was the country with the highest percentage of people living with HIV/AIDS and tuberculosis in the world, the unemployment rate was 40%, and the life expectancy rate at birth was 51 years http://www.immigration-usa.com/world_fact_book_2012/swaziland/index.html. I am so thankful that our God of infinite possibilities allowed us a glimpse beyond the statistics to experience smiling brown faces, warm welcoming arms, stronger faith expressed and lived than I've ever seen, stoic resilience in the face of heart- and backbreaking trials, and natural beauty that prompted a visiting American friend to exclaim that surely Swaziland must be the remnants of the Garden of Eden. It is a kingdom of stunning contrasts that challenged me to the depths of my soul, and of people who changed my heart forever.

Swazis know how a king should be approached; every Swazi living has only lived under kings, and there is a definite protocol and obeisance demanded. Thus they also know how to approach the King of kings—with reverence, honor, and awe. That is how I am approaching this book. I am a fallible human being, relying on my memory, journals and emails to family and friends. I only dare to speak of my King because I know Him and desire to glorify Him. May you also come to know Him through these pages in deeper ways, and be awed by who He is.

Chapter 1

From Travertine to Linoleum

God is the Vinedresser.

...Every branch that bears fruit He prunes, that it may bear more fruit. John 15:2

"Think of the possibilities," our host pastor encouraged nervously as we all attempted to peer through impossibly grimy windows at garbage-strewn floors, walls with peeling paint, broken windows, and ghastly cobwebs everywhere. Frankly, I am not a visionary, and I could not imagine anything at that point due to the lurching of my stomach at the mere thought of living in such squalor. We'd just sold our beautiful, 5-bedroom home in Phoenix, Arizona. I consoled myself with the observation that at least there was flooring intact. As my husband later quipped, we went from "travertine to linoleum."

I was definitely relieved when we all piled in the car and headed back over the bumpy dirt road to the pastor's modern and spotlessly clean home where we were blessed to stay until the workmen could complete what I thought to be an impossible task--making that house from my worst nightmares into a decent home where we would live. It was an unsettling beginning to the Lord's even more unsettling work in my heart as He began to refine me in ways more painful and more glorious than I could ever have envisioned.

He literally and figuratively turned my world upside down. It seemed as though everything I knew, everything I counted on, everything I perceived as solid and real and normal was suddenly and irrevocably topsy-turvy.

I have never been the best of drivers, and now here I was expected to learn to drive on the left side of the street in a vehicle in which the steering wheel was on the right side. It's a good thing this city girl was simultaneously plunked down into a remote rural area with very little traffic. It was quite disconcerting however to go from dodging six lanes of traffic on the freeway in my former life to dodging cows and goats on rough dirt roads that either churned up choking, blinding dust during the dry season, or produced mud that clung to my tires and caused me to be stuck countless times during the rainy season.

Another flip-flop–I have always loved everything seasonal. My husband loved to laugh at my color-coordinated closet where I had my pastels for spring, my earth tones for fall, and lots of thick, long-sleeved Christmas-themed sweaters. It seems silly now, but I was thoroughly discombobulated to suddenly find myself in the Southern Hemisphere where the fall months were March, April, and May, and where Christmas was in the summer. Whatever was I supposed to wear?

Many other foundations were ripped from under me, some superficial, like going from one of the largest and wealthiest nations in the world to one of the smallest and poorest, or from the dry desert where I was raised to a humid subtropical climate. I was challenged to master not only siSwati, but also an entirely different form of English (that spoken by the British colonists of half a century before and still lingering), with a little Afrikaans, Shangan, and Portuguese thrown into the mix of surprising cultural diversity in my new country of residence.

I also learned that what I previously had viewed as a beautiful animal to be enjoyed for its grace (the impala) was cherished far more by some of my new friends for something more sinister to my cloistered sensibilities. I was driving some villagers to a prayer meeting early on when one of these lovely creatures darted out in front of us. Before I could make a social blunder and comment on its aesthetic value, one of the men in the car leapt out of the still-moving car to make chase. For those who are forever starved for any form of protein in their diets, it is simply meat. This lesson, of course, made my complaints seem petty in comparison -- having to travel 90 minutes to a "real" grocery store, or having the electricity and/or running water and/or Internet (yet one more rude awakening--no more high speed--we were back to the dark ages and dial up!) down as much as it was running.

Speaking of grocery stores, I came from a world of Windex, Comet, and Clorox. When our host was out of town one day, her housekeeper asked us to go to the store to get some Handy Andy, Vim, and Jik. To this day she doesn't understand our utter confusion and dismay in that moment over not having a clue how to fulfill our assigned task! We've since learned the names of many other helpful products, some similar to those sold in the US and some even better.

We were often startled at the vast cultural differences in personal modesty. It was nothing for the pastor to announce from the pulpit that congregants must use the inside toilets only rather than urinating on the side of the building. Of course, this was surprising to the men present who thought nothing of emptying their bladders on the side of the road in plain view of passersby. Most do not have the luxury of indoor plumbing or toilets, and children and adults alike had to be trained.

Another pulpit admonition was for the women to cover their breasts while feeding their children. I've always been an advocate for women being able to discretely breastfeed in public, but I have to admit it took some getting used to when women unashamedly bared all when their wee ones needed nourishment. I had to get over any wifely insecurities quickly when it came to my husband. He was far more abashed than I, however, when we were sitting side by side, individually praying for patients at a clinic provided by a team of visiting medical professionals. A pretty young mother he was leading in a prayer of salvation didn't hesitate to reveal all when her infant began to whimper during such a sacred moment. John, being the godly man he is, quickly asked for God to keep his mind where it needed to be!

More profound differences led me to intense, soul-searching, hungry devouring of God's Word like never before, and desperate prayers for understanding and comfort. For example, our home church in the U.S. is quietly Calvinist while our new church was wildly Armenian and made the charismatic churches I'd been in seem tame by comparison.

Another radical paradigm shift with which I was confronted was economics. I'd been raised a proud American, believing with all my heart in my limited understanding of the principles of democracy, the free market system, and the work ethic. Now I was plunked down in a nation ruled by a king. Hard work was rarely rewarded by any shred of material success. So many of those I came to love live on the verge of starvation in spite of doing backbreaking labor just to survive.

One adaptation that was particularly difficult for me was a cultural one. In America (their name for the USA), I could pridefully walk and talk as fast as anyone, and I cherished The Clock and The Calendar which ruled my world. I was gently reminded time and time again in my new home that walking too fast is considered rude, and that I needed to speak much more slowly so people could understand me with my heavy accent. As well, I was patiently taught that relationships and taking time with people are far more important than making the next appointment on time. In other words, I shouldn't complain that a wedding that was scheduled to start at 10 AM didn't begin until noon. I was the only one who was surprised!

This concept of relationships being valued above punctuality also played out as our new home was being refurbished. We were told by the Swazi workers (who would never say anything to your face that you didn't want to hear because that would be horribly rude) that the house would be ready "next week." What we didn't understand was that "next week" would continue to be "next week" for almost two months! One of the first words I learned in siSwati was *kubekethela*, "patience."

As I was grappling with all of this, and the center of my physical, cultural, intellectual, and emotional universe was radically shifting, I alternated between being shaken to the core and being breathlessly exhilarated. It was all a grand adventure and I repeatedly looked at the map trying to adjust to the fact that I was not just geographically around the world but in every other way conceivable as well.

I have absolutely no idea how missionaries of the past handled all of this, because I felt as though I'd be lost without the Internet (albeit intermittent and painfully slow) and constant access to communication with "the real world." I clung to my email connections with friends and family back home as though I were just on vacation and would soon return to reality as I knew it.

One day the Lord quietly corrected me in His Word. I was reading in Philippians 3:13-14: *...But one thing I do: forgetting those things which are behind and reaching forward to those things which are ahead, I press toward the goal....*" A familiar verse was made fresh by the power and teaching of the Holy Spirit, who lovingly guided me to see that I was clinging to life as I used to know it rather than clinging to Jesus and the life He had for me in the present.

At first I was pridefully resistant. "But Lord, we've already given up so much--our home, our careers, our families, and friends. Surely You can't expect more?" Yet He did; He does.

He expects us to die to self, and yes, to suffer with Him. But He gives us so very much more in return.

The trumpet call that day was louder in my heart than the vuvuzelas, those annoyingly blaring instruments used at the World Cup games going on in South Africa at the same time as our arrival. They will forever be the sound I associate with moving to Africa! As I surrendered my heart once again, He opened my eyes to unfathomable blessings.

I came to think of the Internet, electricity, and running water as "The Big Three," and a good day was when all three were actually working. Those things were unpredictable and unreliable, but I was slowly learning to depend on a faithful, dependable Father in ways I know I never would have if He had never called me out of my comfort zones and brought me to a new place of total reliance on Him alone.

As I acquiesced, oh how He blessed me. One of my precious translators gave me the Swazi name of "Siphiwe" which means "gift." Of course, I cried when she christened me with such sweetness. But the truth is, the gift was all mine.

Before we left Arizona, as we were sharing with our shocked acquaintances what God had called us to do, many had never heard of Swaziland, and we got many a chuckle as people either seriously or jokingly misunderstood us and responded, "Where? Switzerland? Disneyland?" No, Swaziland.

One of our new friends was Abraham, a man with the most simple, childlike faith in God I've ever known. His warm words still resonate in my heart today. "Welcome home." Yes, Swaziland was my new...home.

Chapter 2

No More Chickens in the Car!

God is Gracious.

And God is able to make all grace abound toward you, that you, always having all sufficiency in all things, may have an abundance for every good work. 2 Corinthians 9:8

We began to settle in, and I was feeling quite proud of myself as my new translator and I were leaving a community in which we'd just held what I felt was quite a successful women's Bible study. I had managed a few words of siSwati with the group, knew my way to and from the remote area, and was beginning to feel as though I knew what I was doing.

It started sprinkling just as Fikile asked if we could make a "quick stop" so she could take home a chicken for dinner. I'd been in Swaziland long enough to know she didn't mean the grocery store, but didn't want to offend her, so I clamped down on my squeamishness at the ever-present reminder that meat no longer came in neatly-wrapped packages from the cold section of the supermarket.

Regaining my composure and once again feeling pretty good about myself for being so adaptable, I agreed. When we arrived at the home of the woman selling her chickens, a typical lengthy discussion began about the price, and more importantly, about how to transport the wee birdie. Did I have a box? No? Hmm, well, maybe this plastic bag would work. The poor squawking chicken had its legs summarily forced through two quickly-pierced holes in the said bag. I assumed that this was a normal procedure and didn't want to seem ignorant, so allowed the poor frightened fowl to be none-too-gently placed in the back of my vehicle, all the while trying unsuccessfully to ignore the fact that I was an accessory to its imminent grisly murder.

The rain had begun to come down in earnest as we finally got back in the car for the 45-minute journey back home. I was thankful that the downpour on the roof of the car and the booming thunder mostly drowned out the pathetic whimpering and cooing of the terrified hen, but soon learned why the bag had been placed like an ill-fitting, rustling skirt around her. When chickens are mortally afraid, they do what we all would do, and it stank! There was no relief as the torrential rain would have immediately drenched us and the inside of the vehicle if we'd tried to roll down the windows even a crack.

I was never so glad to divest my car of its occupants in my life! I refused to even pretend to be okay at this point, and staunchly remained in the driver's seat while Fikile wrestled with the smelly, traumatized bird, unceremoniously tossing it on the ground. The tension broke as we dissolved into fits of laughter, watching the now partially-liberated-but-still-plastic-skirted hen madly tottering about, trying to rid herself of her putrid costume. I had no idea that my ordeal was not quite over and I drove away in relief.

I had another 15 minutes or so to our house to process all that had just happened, and to come to the conclusion that my darling husband might not find it all so amusing, especially given that the car still seemed to have a residual odor. I hadn't quite come up with what I felt was a suitable way to explain to him that none of it was my fault when I pulled in front of our house and realized he was outside waiting. I never quite got the words out of my mouth. The moment he opened the back of the car to help me retrieve my belongings, we both noticed that the plastic bag had not quite done the trick. I knew that it was best that I just silently agree at that point as he quietly but firmly commanded, "Kay, you will never transport a live chicken in this vehicle again."

Regrettably, he was oblivious to the need to caution me against other critters. It never failed to unnerve me and fill me with revulsion the countless times I reached into a closet or cupboard and came into unwelcome contact with the creepy feeling of a spider web. I mean, yeah, we had spiders in Arizona, of course. But you've never truly encountered spiders until you've confronted and dwelt with African spiders. During the hot season, it was my personal crusade to keep our home web-free, though I confess to utter defeat as the spiders spun many indoor webs each day.

But nothing prepared me for the horror of the morning I left early to pick up my usual carload of vehicle-less neighbors to transport them to church. Please keep in mind that "I am not a morning person" is an understatement when it comes to me. As I drowsily flopped down into the driver's seat and reached for the seatbelt, my horrified senses sprung into alert and eventually my sleep-fogged brain caught on. There was a spider web. All over my seatbelt. All over my steering wheel. All across my dashboard and windshield. I did the only thing a God-fearing, arachnophobic city girl could. I screeched...and then I prayed. And I tell you the truth--I felt the immediate peace that passes all understanding as the Creator of all things, even spiders, gave me the strength to carry on, to clear away the webs, and to praise Him gratefully and loudly that day.

Then there was the Night of the Flying Ants, as it came to be known in our family. The three of us were relaxing together in our tiny living room during the rainy season when the familiar sounds of howling wind, booming thunder, and plopping raindrops on our corrugated metal roof alerted us that yet another storm was upon us. Thunder and lightning are definitely not my thing, but what happened next completely distracted me even from that terror.

My son noticed them initially, as first one, then another and another landed on his neck. It was my turn next and we were both frantically swatting the as-yet-to-be-specified insects off our twitching bodies while my husband looked bemusedly on. Only seconds later he, too, sprang into action as we looked on, horrified at hundreds of flying ants covering the ceiling, the furniture, and the floors. Flyswatters and shoes were wielded as weapons and the three of us thrashed about frantically defending our turf. Thanks to years of experiencing the resounding faithfulness of the Lord, I had the presence of mind to call upon my Defender in battle, even though this battle *was* definitely against flesh and blood. He never fails, and we were victorious! We fell into bed exhausted after the fray, but were greeted with a ghastly reminder of our dominion of the night before when we opened our eyes in the morning to thousands of dead ants littering our home. Triumph comes in many guises, but it is triumph nevertheless!

On another memorable summer evening, I was battling the water beetles covering the screen on our front door while taking one of our dogs out for his evening constitutional. Through trial and error, we'd learned it was far better to leave the outside lights off until we were ready to go bed because any number (and by "any number" I mean countless thousands!) of ghastly African bugs were attracted to the glow. Lamentably I'd forgotten that discipline this particular night and had a veritable army awaiting me. My pup was beginning to get desperate so I hastily opened the door trying to let in as few clicking beetles as possible and whacked my way back through the hordes after he'd done his duty in the yard.

Once back into the perceived safety of the house, I noticed an itchy feeling on my back and naturally began to slap my skin trying to reach the irritated spot just out of reach. Bad move--I felt a distinct "crunch," and when I queasily asked my ever-patient husband to investigate, he displayed the crushed remains he'd confiscated from my back. Ick. The casual comment tossed off by several American friends of, "I could never move to Africa because I don't like bugs," kept running through my mind. Let me make this clear. Do you think I do?! This time it took a lot of prayer to achieve peaceful slumber, but God is good and sleep finally came.

Even the most patient of husbands get mischievous once in a while. Yet another summertime evening was in progress. On such a beautiful, clear night, we were outside gazing at the plethora of stars extravagantly revealed in the dark African bush so far away from any city lights, a pleasure that never ceased to delight and amaze us. Apparently the resident bats were enjoying the evening as well and became quite friendly. Before I knew it, they were literally encircling my head in some sort of macabre bat dance. Yep, I screamed and beat a hasty retreat inside, followed by my husband's loud chuckles. His Facebook post the next morning read, "I'm sorry for laughing at you last night while the bats were flying around your head." Humph.

So often we had to laugh or we'd cry. One of those instances was when an American visiting our pastor had asked to hear how we came to serve the Lord as full-time missionaries. We are always eager to share what God has done in our lives and began the tale. Before long, the guest interrupted with what was presumably an unthinking comment. She passionately proclaimed that she could never serve full-time on the mission field because she loves her family too much. On so many levels this agitated me; did she think we loved our families less? I called on the Lord to give me the self-control not to respond out of my hurt. I wanted to shout to her about the hours of weeping we'd done saying goodbye to our elderly parents and older son. I wanted to vehemently describe the daily sorrow we carry around missing our loved ones back in America. Most of all, I wanted to defend our decision to follow Jesus at great personal cost, because we love Him most.

Always gracious, the Lord held me back, showing me that I was being prideful and easily offended. As my heartbeat gradually returned to normal, I also realized that this dear woman might never be graced with the raw beauty and joy that comes with full surrender to Christ, and I thanked Him then and there for allowing us to follow Him wherever He leads.

So here we are in Africa. Just in case you've missed the glaring clues so far, I suffer from Obsessive Compulsive Disorder. You might ask the same question those who know me well have asked, and indeed the question I used to ask myself. Why would a sovereign, wise and loving Father send his squeamish, highly sensitive, germ-phobic daughter to rural Africa of all places? The answer as I've come to know it is powerful, startling, and magnificent. I survive here because of, and only because of, His unlimited and glorious grace, which is all I need. Is it easy? Not a chance. Does He sustain me and fortify me and work through my weaknesses for His great glory? Absolutely!

In the early days I struggled to adjust to my new less-than-hygienic environment. I was wrestling with a fleshly desire to go back to the more pristine surroundings of our former life in an exclusive suburb of Phoenix. I thank God for my friend and mentor who quietly reminded me in the midst of my pity party that the very Son of God left the perfect heavenly realms to come as a poor baby to this fallen earth with all its squalor and filth, extraordinarily because He loves us so much. I knew in that moment that my meager sacrifice paled in comparison, and began to embrace His limitless grace poured out on me. It was--and is--more than enough.

One of the tremendous perks of being a missionary is that it is expected that you spend lots and lots of time in God's Word. In my former career, I was hard-pressed to carve out my daily time for His life-giving Bread. But now, what was once a hard-won luxury became part of the job description! It was no coincidence that during this time the Holy Spirit guided me to that timeless comfort found in 2 Corinthians 12:9: *"...'My grace is sufficient for you, for My strength is made perfect in weakness.' Therefore most gladly I will rather boast in my infirmities that the power of Christ may rest upon me."*

My dear friend Margaret came to visit us each year and both she and the women in my Bible study groups found great delight in her sharing the Word with them each time she came. One year, her message included the powerful phrase, "But God," which is translated in siSwati, "Kodvwa Nkulunkulu." This term is found repeatedly in the Bible, and Margaret found creative ways to help us remember "Kodvwa Nkulunkulu," including waving in the air laminated Scripture cards whenever she read a verse with the same statement. For years afterwards, we'd cheerfully remind each other in times of trials,

"But God." Ephesians 2:4-5 *But God, being rich in mercy, because of the great love with which He loved us, even when we were dead in our trespasses, made us alive together with Christ!* Oh, how I can vouch for the veracity of this divine Truth! To You alone, my gracious King, be all the honor and glory.

Chapter 3

Meshach and Abednego, Minus Shadrach

God is Sovereign.

> *...It is not in man who walks to direct his own steps.*
> Jeremiah 10:23

One thing that became indubitably indisputable in my soul through serving Him on the mission field is that God is sovereign and there are no coincidences. In Isaiah 55:9 God tells us, *"For as the heavens are higher than the earth, so are My ways higher than your ways…"* And oh, how much better as well! Time and again while I had ideas of how the day should go, He delighted me by revealing His infinitely better plans.

On one such occasion John, two young Swazi helpers from our church and I set out to get photos and names of about 100 children to register them for sponsors for a feeding program. As you can imagine, it was enchanting but chaotic work corralling and documenting one adorable, sweaty child after another, and it took us most of the day. Thankfully, much of our work took place in the local schools, and the teachers did their best to help us.

Two delightful young boys were in line together, and we were told that they were twins named Meshach and Abednego. I asked if there was a Shadrach and was met by quizzical looks from the boys and teachers alike. Once I discerned that none of them knew the story from which the boys' names originated, I knew on the spot that I was to share the story from the Bible found in Daniel, chapter 3. I was grateful that in Swaziland, Christianity is still embraced in the schools. Dozens of teachers and about 50 children gathered around to hear the tale of three young courageous men whose faith in God underwent a severe test, and who, in the process, gave glory and honor to the Lord who walks with us in the fire, and saves us from it. It was an exquisite moment in time, bathed in the almost-palpable glow of the Holy Spirit, as we commissioned the boys to be godly men of valor like their namesakes.

John and I inadvertently began teaching another lesson early on. We had only been in Swaziland a week or so, but determinedly persevered in our cherished practice of having a date night together once a week, no matter what else was going on in our lives. I truly believe this ritual has contributed greatly to keeping our marriage together through hard times and good, as has our tradition of praying together every night.

In Africa, due to a lifestyle committed to frugality, date night often simply meant taking popcorn and driving to one of a gazillion deserted rows between sugar cane fields. We would park and eat and talk in the enchanted setting of crystal clear skies adorned with billions of sparkling stars, twinkling fireflies flitting all around our car, and cicadas singing their buzzing praises to the Most High God.

We were headed out the door on our first such outing in Swaziland when our hostess' housekeeper and her assistant-in-training asked us where we were going. When we explained that for almost our entire marriage we had dates once a week, we were baffled by their responses of giggles, sly grins, and utter disbelief. In their experience, men simply did not "date" their wives, ever. Once a man paid lobola (bride price of cows) for his wife, he virtually owned her as property and in his thinking, to treat her to a date would be ludicrous and unnecessary. The two housekeepers, one old and jaded and one young but coming from a horribly abusive relationship, finally settled on being charmed by what John was doing for me.

From this experience we surmised that God would use our marriage as a model of how He intends marriage to be--a loving relationship between a man and a woman, mirroring His own faithful and passionate love towards His bride, the church, and her adoration in response. Time after time, simple acts like John putting his arm around me, or helping me with a heavy load, or serving me a cold drink of water caused bemusement from all watching, and, we dare to hope, a shift in the way at least a few Swazi men treat their wives, and in how many women view their worth to the Lord.

One Swazi husband whose life was truly transformed when he surrendered his life to Jesus was Philemon. Philemon became a cherished friend, taught us much about Swazi culture, and was an incredible example to us of rock-solid faith.

Once he became a Christian, Philemon immediately gave up his philandering lifestyle and concentrated on being the best husband and father he could be to his two wives (polygamy is not only legal but embraced in Swazi culture) and a dozen or so children. This large family barely eked out an existence with subsistence farming. Philemon and both his wives were also HIV+ and reliant on antiretroviral medication to fight opportunistic diseases.

Early one morning Philemon appeared at our door asking if we could give him some money as his wife needed to take public transportation to the hospital about a 90-minute drive away for an important medical appointment. We were unable at that time to help him, and he graciously accepted the news and declared in total faith that God would make a way. God is a rewarder of faith, and surely enough, it came about that a neighbor was also headed to the hospital and could take Philemon's wife, Lomcwasho, along for the ride.

We were already rejoicing in God's provision when He revealed His even greater plan for the day. Had John and I been able to give Philemon the money earlier in the day, Lomcwasho would have missed entirely the drama that occurred when she arrived at the hospital later that afternoon. One of Philemon's former girlfriends was there with the daughter they'd produced in his days of unrestrained sexual behaviors. The mother was in the process of getting the young girl admitted to the hospital because she was very sick with meningitis, one of the opportunistic diseases to which those who are HIV+ are prone. When the poor mother, who was sick and starving herself, saw

Lomcwasho, she begged her to take the girl home with her upon her release from the hospital, as she could no longer take care of her herself. Though this child was a product of her husband's infidelity, Lomcwasho, with Christ-like compassion, agreed to take her in as her own and raise her to serve the Lord. The girl survived, grew to love Jesus and became active in the church youth group, thanks to Lomcwasho's utterly selfless act as well as God's providential plan for the girl's life.

~

Sadly, godly men like Philemon are in the minority, and the rape of children and women is widespread. According to one study published by the United States National Library of Medicine National Institutes of Health, approximately "thirty-two percent of respondents reported an incident of sexual violence before they reached 18 years of age (http://www.ncbi.nlm.nih.gov/pubmed/19428100). Especially in the frequent cases of incest, it is rarely reported. The cultural norm, according to the over 60 Swazi women I interviewed, is to "keep things in the family," so far too many children are exhorted to just keep quiet about abuse. But God knows, and God sees, and God cares.

One of my primary tools of ministry was teaching stories of women in the Bible to women in the villages, with life-application lessons and discussion at the end of each session. It was my passion to share the life-changing Word of God to the mostly illiterate women who are raising the next generation of Swazis, with the hope that His precepts will transform the culture to His Kingdom culture. Each day when I woke up, I sought Him as to which story I should teach that day. Often the answer I got was not the answer I wanted or thought best, but He is patient with my reticence and I was always astounded when I complied and saw His wisdom for that day, for that group of women.

On one particular day I felt strongly that I was to teach the sad and ugly story of Tamar, daughter of King David, who was raped by her half-brother. While the biblical account is straightforward and leaves the casual reader with feelings of disgust and hopelessness, any student of the Bible knows that some of its prevailing themes include hope, restoration, and goodness, and I make it a point to incorporate these themes in the lesson of Tamar, concluding with Isaiah 61:1-3, the glorious passage about bringing beauty from ashes.

It is not my favorite story to share due to its disturbing content; however, I have learned to listen to the Holy Spirit. Even though I was tired and wished for a "happier" tale to relate, we dove into the history of the atrocity committed upon Tamar. The normally aloof and impassive group of ladies became obviously more agitated as the drama unfolded, and I soon learned the reason behind their unusual behavior. Swazi women are so used to too much death, too much suffering, and too much abuse that they are typically very stoic, even with each other, and rarely voice their pain.

Thanks be to God that He opened the floodgates that day as the women related that the five-year-old daughter of one of the group members had come to her mother the night before with the horrific report that an uncle has been systematically sexually abusing her. Because of God's living and active Word, we had a timely and profound discussion, and were able to encourage the mother to report the abuse to the proper authorities and help her to help her precious daughter.

Crime happens all too often; the miracle is how God redeems situations. It was my joy to be able to distribute donated Bibles to those who otherwise could not afford them. Over the years we've been able to give out hundreds of Bibles, always with the admonition that they are not to be sold to buy the next meal, or to be used as toilet paper, since Swazis simply use whatever paper they can find on the ground or anywhere else for this purpose. Our prayer is always that the Bibles will be cherished and read regularly.

As part of one session training women in Moms in Prayer International (MIPI) prayer to lift up their children and local schools in intercession, I gave the group leader about ten Bibles to share with prospective members who were not able to come that day. Several weeks passed and I felt led to check back in to see how the group was going. After the usual formal courtesies followed by the typically indirect innuendo that something was amiss, I was finally able to grasp what was being politely (never rudely and directly!) implied. The treasured Bibles had been stolen by a mentally unstable and criminal son. The poor woman was horrified to have to communicate this to me and was obviously ashamed and even fearful of what my response would be.

She was visibly taken aback with my immediate smile and even quiet giggling. I quickly explained that there were still more Bibles available with which I could replace the stolen ones. But more than that, I told her that the God we serve is sovereign, and I believed with all my heart that He would see to it that those pilfered Bibles would wind up in the hands of those who needed them most, who otherwise might not have ever had one. We prayed right then and there, thanking God for His purposes for those Bibles and trusting Him with the outcome. I know my friend received a valuable lesson that day through the orchestration of a wise Master Planner.

On top of our regular more-than-full days of ministry, we often entertained guests, both invited and uninvited. I was often quietly amused to remember how virtually no one came to visit us when we lived in inhospitably hot Phoenix, Arizona, and yet now that we'd moved all the way across the world to such an exotic locale, there seemed to be a constant flow of travelers. Some genuinely wanted to spend time with us and we were exceedingly grateful for their sacrificial time and generosity in coming to taste a little of our new world and to minister to those we'd come to love deeply in Swaziland.

I confess to being a little less gracious in my heart towards complete strangers who knew someone who knew someone who knew us and who wished to stay with us for "just a day or two" while passing through. My ever-patient Teacher always reminded me that these times were priceless opportunities to expose others to the mission He had given us to share Jesus with a lost and dying population.

I cannot even remember what the connection was to one kind American couple, other than that they were accompanying their college-aged son who would be studying in Swaziland in the upcoming year through some sort of exchange program. We offered to show them "our" little corner of the "real" Swaziland for the short few hours they'd be in our area and they were excited at the prospect. He was a professional photojournalist and gleefully snapped away while her attention was mostly diverted to a young girl (the daughter of our friend, Jane), who has cerebral palsy and simply crawled around in the dirt and muck to get around in her small village of mud huts and severe poverty.

We knew right away that it was no coincidence that our visitors were there, at that time, in that place of suffering, to bless this precious child. It turned out that their own daughter also has cerebral palsy, and the American mother was appalled at the discrepancy between the services afforded her daughter in the wealthy USA versus the utter lack of help for "Sister" in rural Swaziland. It took many, many emails back and forth, but after several painstaking weeks, this generous one-day visitor changed the lives not only of Sister, but also of her mother.

Jane had believed that no one cared, and that she was on her own to provide for her daughter as the father was deceased. She learned that day that God Almighty Himself cared enough to send a middle-class mother from the other side of the world to purchase a specially-designed wheelchair from a company in a large city in the neighboring country of South Africa.

We experienced sheer joy when finally, my husband, after hours of frustration trying to follow the inevitable indecipherable instructions for putting the contraption together, successfully completed the process. Sister gestured wildly and exclaimed loudly over and over for all to hear that God had given her own "car!" That triumphant day she became part of the community that previously had either ignored her, or worse, shunned her, due to the superstitious belief that those with disabilities were carriers of a curse. The other children vied for their turn to push Sister around while the entire village came out to see the gleeful commotion. Smile after smile broke out on their long-suffering countenances.

Usually visitors who came from the US wanted to shop for souvenirs, mostly inexpensive trinkets as either mementos or as gifts for supporters who helped pay for their short-term mission trips. A favorite place to take them was an outdoor market with about one hundred stalls, with mostly women selling merchandise. Some visitors flitted randomly to various stalls, some entered the first two or three they came to and then settled on their purchases, and some systematically tried each and every stall to bargain for the best deals. Since I am not a shopper, this process is frankly onerous to me, and I grieve seeing how hard these poor women fight for each and every sale to support their families.

One balmy day I was halfheartedly trying to keep up with our browsing friends, who were obviously in no hurry and thoroughly enjoying the process. John was close behind me, ready to help with the bargaining or to step in if someone tried to take advantage of our guests. I entered yet another tiny stall with poorly-made items and the stuffy smell of sweaty bodies and mildew.

Instantly though, I knew that this time, and this woman, were different. Like countless others, this woman was hungry and lost, but this was her day. I'm not a comfortable evangelist, but the Holy Spirit's presence was so strong and the message so clear that I was supposed to ask this young mother if she knew Jesus as her Lord and Savior. She replied in good English (thankfully, as my siSwati was woefully inadequate at that time for such an enormous undertaking!) that she knew who Jesus was and wanted to surrender to Him, but that she needed to put some things in her life in order before becoming a Christian. My husband and I grinned at each other while I quickly and passionately reassured her that she did not have to live a perfect life before coming to Jesus, and that He died for her sins, and wanted her as His own daughter right then, in that moment, and that He Himself would help her to clean up her life. I will never forget the brilliant smile that instantly lit up her round face. I led her in a simple sinner's prayer and warmly hugged her as I welcomed her into the family of Christ and as my spiritual sister.

We visited the market several months later and had barely stepped foot outside our car when an exuberant Judith came racing across the dusty dirt expanse between us and threw herself into my arms with tears of joy. She related how being a child of God had completely changed her life, and we knew beyond a shadow of a doubt that it was true, as her previously downcast countenance now radiated His pure joy. We have kept in touch with her ever since and she continues to passionately pursue her Savior.

Sometimes the Lord does prepare me ahead of time for His plans. Even before we moved to Swaziland, I had a dream of starting a hospital ministry there, but I had absolutely no idea how to walk that out practically. The closest hospital to where we lived was about a 90-minute drive away, and gasoline (or petrol, as it is called here in southern Africa) was not cheap. I had it in my head to just wait until the Lord provided, and until after we'd been in ministry in Swaziland for a while, and I could recruit and train some sort of team.

I had no way of knowing that the Lord had also placed the same dream in the heart of a dear woman in the most unlikely of places. Ncamsile lived in the same mud hut village as Sister, where many often didn't even have enough food to eat. When they did, their diet consisted almost entirely of a corn meal mush known as "pap," with sometimes indigenous green plants to supplement.

I led a Bible study with a group of about 20 women from this community, many of whom also attended Sunday morning services via transportation provided by the local church. One day as we were having our discussion under our regular tree on a particular Bible story with the related theme of giving, Ncamsile gave voice to the desire God had put in her heart. She said many of them truly had nothing to tithe and nothing to give for an offering of monetary value, but that they very much wanted to serve the Lord as a way of tithing and thanking Him.

She then shared her dream of a group of them doing hospital visits to minister to the patients, who often were also so poor that their families could not afford the cost of public transportation to visit them. Tears began to pour from my eyes as I tried to find the words to respond to these precious women, sitting in their tattered clothing on their hand-woven mats in the dirt, who still wanted to serve and love others. At last, I found my voice and explained that Ncamsile's dream echoed my own, and that I was sure that it was also the Lord's plan, but that there were still many obstacles as far as finances and logistics, so they needed to join me in praying for it to come to pass.

We serve a mountain-moving, miracle-working God, and it wasn't long at all before a team was formed, and eight women piled into our two vehicles, and we were off for Good Shepherd Hospital. The others who could not fit formed a prayer group, and interceded for us the whole time we were away. Oh, what a glorious beginning as the ladies sang beautiful siSwati praise and worship songs for the entire hour we were driving, interspersed with prayers for our mission. They were on fire!

John and I told them from the beginning that we were just the drivers, that this was their ministry, and they needed to take charge of it. As Americans, we expected a well-thought-out and executed plan would be predetermined and executed. Once we arrived, the women piled out of the car...and were silent...and stood rooted in place beside our vehicles. After a couple of awkward minutes, I realized they were terrified, and had no idea how to proceed from that point. It took some encouragement, but finally Ncamsile stepped up and suggested we hold hands and pray, and we did. She then instructed two others who could read and who had brought Bibles to find some appropriate verses that they could share. All of this took at least 30 minutes, and began to tax my patience, as well as that of my husband. I know we both wondered if we would ever actually put foot inside the hospital.

I noticed that Ncamsile was trembling with nerves, but it was as though suddenly God Himself strengthened her, and she resolutely began to move forward with purpose, with the others following along like baby chicks behind a mother hen. I promptly christened her "Pastor Chicken" because of this, as well as because of her former timidity, and we all laughed, dissolving some of the tension.

Once we were inside the hospital, I witnessed one of the fastest, most amazing transformations I have ever seen.

Ncamsile, after checking in at the nurses' station (another process that seemed to take forever and once again tested my patience!), began systematically to lead the group from ward to ward. She assigned roles to each member based on their personalities and giftings, while she herself began to preach the Gospel. Loudly. Boldly. Another member passed out the little treats we'd brought, while others went individually from bedside to bedside offering prayers. The unlikely rag-tag band of downtrodden, marginalized women became an awesome force in the hands of the Living God. They led many to the Lord that day, and comforted more than I could count.

Ncamsile became my ministry partner and closest friend, and we experienced a lifetime of God's goodness and miracles and joy and sorrow together in those few short years, but I will never forget that glorious day when "Pastor Chicken" became "Pastor Lion." She was a born leader waiting to be set free, and I was the witness to God's wondrous transformational power.

This chapter would not be complete without mentioning one more chronicle. I was blessed to be on the praise and worship team at our local church. I was the only one on the team with any kind of formal musical training, yet the others were some of the best natural musicians with whom I have ever performed. And oh, how hard they worked to be excellent for their Maker. Rehearsals would last for hours and hours, and the sound guy would labor endlessly and thanklessly to make the antiquated sound system operate smoothly. Often much of rehearsal time was spent trying to find a way to circumvent this or that wire that had been gnawed by the resident rats.

On Sunday mornings, we arrived two hours early; the first hour was devoted to intercessory prayer for the service, and the second hour was devoted to another rehearsal. So much time and effort was poured into our idea of how things should go.... And then at the last minute, as congregants began streaming in the doorway, the electricity would go out. The groans from the team were always loud and resentful as our best-laid plans and practice came to naught. Without the electric keyboard, we could not do the songs we'd planned.

This happened so often that everyone knew their roles, and quickly some of us devised a Plan B list of songs that could easily be sung a Capella by us as well as the congregation. Others procured the candles for light as we were in pitch darkness, while still others checked the circuit breaker (rarely the culprit) and helped the flow of people to their seats in the now-dim lighting from the candles.

Our plans did not always work out, but what followed was one of the most beautiful things I have ever experienced as we sang hauntingly beautiful praise and worship songs to the Lord, with breathtaking, pitch-perfect harmony as can only be experienced in Africa, in the soft glow of the well-worn candles. God's plans, not our own, and they are glorious.

Chapter 4

Stinky Lion Breath

God is our Protector.

...Your adversary the devil walks about like a roaring lion...
1 Peter 5:8

One of the perks of living in Africa is getting to see the famed exotic animals in the wild rather than in a zoo. It never failed to delight me to be forced to stop for a giraffe crossing the road, or to chuckle at a family of warthogs with their tails straight up in the air as they trotted away on their short, stiff legs.

Best of all, when visitors came, it warranted a trip to the nearby game preserve, where we were able to walk among lumbering but seemingly peaceable rhinos, drive breathtakingly close to trumpeting elephants, and if we were lucky, get up close and personal with magnificent lions. Often we would do the game drive near sunset, when the lions were just waking up and stretching, preparing to hunt. I'll never forget the stench of fresh blood as we came upon one pride just after they'd caught an impala. Excitement and horror warred within me at the sight!

As we became veterans of such thrilling forays, we knew that as long as we stayed in the vehicle we were safe, since the lions perceived us as a bigger animal and would not try to attack us. On one such excursion, my companion and I shared the large, open safari vehicle with about eight other people. It was Elizabeth's first time, and obviously the first time as well for the very nervous middle-aged woman in front of us. She spoke in a decidedly peevish British accent to her obviously long-suffering husband, who did his best to placate her.

Our disgruntled fellow passenger became a little less crotchety as we passed delicate impalas, graceful giraffes, and adorable zebras. Just as she seemed to actually begin enjoying our adventure, we came upon one male and two female full-grown lions lounging in the tall grass. We could actually smell their pungent, wild animal odor before we saw them, but when we did lay eyes on them, there were the usual awed "ooh's" and "ahh's" and hushed whispers of delight at actually getting to see these majestic beasts.

As the driver shut the vehicle off so we could more fully enjoy the experience, I could sense our grumpy companion's renewed unease. The rest of us respectfully whispered our delighted comments about the antics of the beasts for many moments before the driver deemed it was time to move on to get back to the camp before the absolute darkness of the African night fell upon us.

He turned the ignition...and nothing happened. He tried again, and again, and again, with the same results. The tension in the vehicle rose quickly, but I whispered to my friend that we were in no danger, explaining what I knew about their unwillingness to tackle the larger "animal" of the safari conveyance. It was still nerve-wracking to be stuck in the middle of the African wild with a trio of gigantic and fully wild felines no more than five feet away from us, and suddenly Elizabeth and I erupted into hysterical giggling. We tried to stifle our untimely snickers and guffaws, but apparently our by-this-time-highly-aggravated vehicle mate turned around and vehemently chastised us to be quiet! This only made us giggle more uncontrollably.

Obviously I survived to tell the thrilling tale, and Elizabeth and I have a shared memory of an exciting time. I only pray that somehow that poor beleaguered woman finds it in her heart to forgive us! I also pray that she comes to know Jesus, and to realize that the true enemy is not a malodorous earthly creature, but rather Satan himself, who comes to "kill, steal, and devour." I thank God that I know He is my ever-present shield and deliverer because there truly was a lot that caused me momentary fear in my new surroundings!

~

There was the report of the python behind the church that was observed devouring, one by one, nine poor defenseless chickens kept on the property. Once he'd finally gotten his fill and moved on, the suffering two survivors refused to come down from the trees for weeks. I confess it was all I could do not to join them in seeking perceived safety!

~

I once had a large mamba, a snake whose venom can kill in a matter of 45 minutes, rise up and strike my moving car. I was trembling so badly that once I reached my destination, I begged the ladies there to check underneath the car before I could pry myself out and shakily conduct the Bible study there.

～

Cobras were frequent visitors to our yard, and we had no recourse but to call our male neighbors who always valiantly came to the rescue. Though they were clearly as fearful as we were, they did possess a lifetime of skills in dealing with snakes that we did not. However, they did learn one trick from my older and wiser husband! Cobras are well-known to spit their venom in opponents' eyes, which can be not only horribly painful but sometimes permanently blinding. Although our neighbors chuckled at John in his safety goggles, the very next time they all wanted to wear them!

My own closest encounter with a scary, slithering serpent happened when I went to teach some preschool teachers and care point cooks (who fed hundreds of hungry children each day with food donated from the US). It was a miserably hot day, and rather than suffer sitting inside in the stifling heat of an un-air-conditioned classroom, we opted to sit outside in the meager but still-present, desultory breeze under a shady canopy.

The ladies always tried to honor me by not allowing me to lift a finger to do manual labor, but I was just as determined to honor them by helping whenever I could, so I followed one of the teachers inside to gather the well-worn and broken plastic chairs on which the group could precariously sit. The chairs were stacked in a corner of the dimly-lit classroom, and in my reckless (and to be honest, maybe a bit prideful) haste to be of service, I rushed headlong towards danger. Nomsa grabbed my arm and unceremoniously jerked me back while simultaneously shrieking, "Cobra, cobra!"

In quick succession, she and I rushed pell-mell outside up onto a low cement wall while the other teacher ran to fetch the young man who did odd jobs around the place. (I have also known women to kill snakes, but in Swaziland there is still a very clear idea of gender-based roles, and snake-killing is deemed men's work, which, for all my high-flown ideals about women's worth and abilities, I am hypocritically thankful!).

My rather impetuous interpreter had no such qualms, however, and excitedly followed the designated snake-killer into the classroom. My companions and I held our collective breath as we heard first a loud "thunk" (which we later were told was the large rock being heaved at the snake), followed by a definite female shriek, once again followed by an even louder "thunk," and yet another piercing scream. After what seemed an eternity but was probably less than a minute, the now-proud hero came out with the thoroughly vanquished enemy draped over the end of a long stick.

As excited chatter ensued, the ladies reliving the story over and over, I silently prayed to the Lord to give me the fortitude to carry on. And He did. And we did. Six women defied the enemy's tactics that day, five were trained in spiritual warfare, and a new Moms in Prayer International (MIPI) group of prayer warriors was born!

Another cobra and another village, and this time it seemed the enemy had won. I arrived to find an elderly woman silently enduring what I am told is excruciating pain from a cobra spitting its venom in her eyes the night before. The snake had entered her mud hut and was hiding in the rubber boot she used in her menial-labor job of weeding the nearby sugar cane fields. When she startled the snake, it reacted swiftly, and she'd been in agony for hours.

I was way out of my element and had no idea what to do, but I had learned to respect the many and assorted survival skills of these simple village women. When I asked, they told me the clinic about 10 kilometers away might have the supplies to help her (supplies were limited and not always dependable), but they still politely refused to directly ask me, as the only one with a vehicle, to assist her. It took me a few minutes to understand that they were indirectly pleading with me for mercy.

Again I had to share my ignorance, urgently wanting to alleviate her suffering at all costs, but having no idea how much money was required for services at the facility. While I had vastly more money with the scant few bills and coins in my bag than they did, my American mind was still programmed to expect a hefty bill for which I would be responsible and could never pay.

Much to my surprise, the cost was literally comparable to US pennies, so the granny and as many others as possible promptly piled into my makeshift "ambulance" and off we went. Appropriate to the granny's suffering state, the women began crooning a soft worship song, while I frantically tried to shift gears, wondering if there was any way, after all the time that was already lost with the crisis, that we could still have our Bible study that I'd spent so much time preparing.

Once again, I confessed my ignorance and asked my interpreter for wisdom. She suggested that since the patient would likely have to wait hours to be seen, we drop her off with a young woman to help her, and return to the community to try to have at least a short Bible study, since all the women there were still expectantly waiting. I agreed, but was secretly frustrated because I knew my well-laid plans would come to naught, and I'd be able to fit in an abbreviated version of the lesson at best before nightfall, when it would be too dangerous for me to be in the village.

It was only months later that I realized the full import of that day. While I had been frustrated that my plans were sabotaged, God was working His perfect plan. Not only was He teaching me important lessons in trusting Him and not depending on my foolish pride and inept abilities, He was also forging a real relationship between the village women and me. This relationship became something deep and abiding and joyous because of the trials He enabled us to face together, rather than the smooth and happy times together I'd envisioned. The granny fully recovered after our fervent joint prayers for her, and a lifelong bond was forged.

Snakes and lions were far from the only mortal creatures to be dreaded. Death in Africa comes from animals as small as a malaria-carrying mosquito to an aggravated hippopotamus. However, the beast I came to abhor the most was the Nile crocodile. This monstrous amphibian was responsible for more deaths of people I knew personally than any other animal.

Once again I ignorantly and clumsily blundered into my first knowledge of the horror with which my new friends viewed the crocs they encountered in the river. This was the very river from which they had to fetch water to drink, wash clothes, do dishes, and bathe. Before each Bible study, I liked to do "ice breaker" questions, and carelessly thought the lists of questions I found online, likely written by city-dwelling Americans like I used to be, would suffice brilliantly. I thought I was quite smart in deleting the obviously incongruent questions like, "What is your favorite movie?" since none of them had seen a movie in their entire lives.

One particular day early on, I eagerly anticipated their answers to, "What is your favorite animal," and even envisioned giving some sparkling analogies from the animal kingdom to the spiritual one. I was a bit taken aback by their rather practical answers, such as, "chickens, because they are good to eat." My worldview shifted even more abruptly though when one mother matter-of-factly told me instead that her least favorite animal was a crocodile, because one had eaten her young child a few years ago. Oh, I still had so very much to learn about their silent suffering, and still so very much to learn about their amazing, resilient trust in God's protection in their lives.

This same group of resolute women feared something far more than crocodiles; they feared sickness. In a country where everyone has lost at least one close family member to AIDS, but where few are educated enough to understand the disease, every cough and every low-grade fever were cause for dread, and cause for fervent prayer to the only Healer they had. I learned this the hard way as well.

I had a pretty bad case of bronchitis, and decent medical care was two and a half hours and a country away in South Africa, so I was just trying to sleep and sweat it off at home. I was miserable, but in my American security from a lifetime of great and accessible medical care, was positively certain I'd survive. I sent a message to all my Bible study groups that I would be unable to come that week due to being ill, and climbed promptly back into my pity party and my bed.

It was only a few weeks later when I was finally able to return to work that I learned that all had been fervently praying for me. One group had even spent several sleepless nights in intercession for my life. Once again, I was profoundly humbled; I offered them two hours a week of my time while they offered me so very, very much more.

～

Among those who knew me, it became a joke about how many times I got stuck in the mud. The rutted dirt roads we traveled on became true quagmires during the rainy season, and in spite of much patient instruction by anyone and everyone about how to identify the best place to pass when there was deep water across the whole road, I never did master the skill.

Our friend Philemon, who did not have a driver's license but who often gallantly helped me out of each messy episode with his innate abilities, became a bit weary of my incompetence, I think. When I once again called him to the rescue, he sent his "tribe" of ten children out in the pouring rain to assist, and only leisurely followed behind to coach them. I had to laugh when I saw the kids all running full tilt around the bend in the road, subsequently having a blast jumping into the knee-deep mud to push me out while a chuckling Philemon directed from the drier side of the road.

I had become complacent, believing I would always have someone to help me out of my puddles in life, and carelessly dependent on my husband and friends, forgetting where my true help lies. So one day when John and Jeremy were in South Africa for a medical trip, and without contemplating the fact that Philemon and others I casually relied on were also all away, I confidently set out to teach a Bible study. When I came across a large body of water across my route, I did what I always did. I took a deep breath, prayed, and began to plow through (proud of remembering to keep the car in a low gear as I'd been taught, and not stop).

I got a familiar sinking feeling in my stomach at the same time I felt my vehicle literally sinking into the muck. Swazi mud, at least where we lived, is a rich red clay--beautiful to look at, but disastrous in which to be stuck. I am not known for my cool-headedness, and this time was no different. I frantically spun my wheels, only to sink deeper. In my increasing panic, I used up precious cell phone battery time to call person after person I knew were all too far away to come. I was in the middle of rural Swaziland, in between two fields of sugar cane much taller than I, with no one for many, many miles.

Or so I thought, when suddenly a machete-wielding cane cutter appeared out of the bush. I could now taste real fear as horror story after horror story came rushing back to me of how white people's body parts are valued for their magical properties by witch doctors, and of the many women I'd known who had been brutally raped in this area. Cane cutters are strong men who work for almost nothing and are often more desperate than even I felt at that moment.

To my amazement he cautiously approached and began speaking in siSwati, which I barely comprehended at that time, and gesturing that he would help me. I had no choice but to helplessly watch as he began cutting brush and placing it under my tires. I sent many frenzied prayers up begging for help out of my predicament, while guardedly keeping an eye on my unlikely rescuer, hoping he wouldn't suddenly decide to murder me for my body parts instead. It was beyond my worst nightmares when he flagged down another filth-encrusted, disreputable-looking man, who was also carrying the compulsory machete, to assist in his efforts.

Time passed slowly as branch after branch was laboriously cut and strategically placed. My high-level of tension couldn't sustain itself, so I resignedly did as they indicated when they finally motioned, and started my engine and tried to move forward, but to no avail. The second man, likely already exhausted after a hard day's labor in the fields, gave up and went on his way. But the first man was clearly not leaving my side, whether I wanted him to or not. After an excruciating time of inability to communicate more than a few words in each other's language, neither of us having a clue as to what to do next, I resumed my desperate prayers.

On this rarely-traveled road, we suddenly saw a truck approaching us, with yet another unknown man driving. I was almost deliriously happy when he shouted out his window, in good English, that he would also try to help. I was beyond my fear of strange men at that point and just wanted to get out of that tenacious mud trap. The new man, who had a young boy in the truck with him, seemed less threatening to me, so when he offered to take me somewhere to get help, I gratefully agreed. The first man, this illiterate field hand, showing more grace than most supposed "gentlemen" I've ever met, chopped down yet more branches with his field knife and waded in the knee-deep mud to position them by my driver's side door in a valiant attempt to keep me from muddying my skirt. In spite of his noble gesture, my first step out of the vehicle was into the same quagmire of filth, and I waded my ungraceful way to the new man's truck and clambered in.

As only God can orchestrate, it turned out that the truck owner was a cousin to one of my friends in the village where I asked him to take me to get help. My women friends all scrambled to find a rope and after about 45 minutes, miraculously a nice long, strong one was found. My dear friend Ncamsile refused to let me get back into the vehicle alone with the man, and determinedly got in with me. It was only when we were on the approximately 15-minute ride back to my car that I realized that I'd left the car door wide open with my purse, phone, and money on the front seat completely exposed. I was certain I would return to find them all gone; after all, the people in this part of the country lived in abject poverty, and this amount of wealth could sustain a family for a month. I believed it was only the mud that would keep my vehicle from also being stolen, because I'd left my keys in the ignition.

My self-centered, ego-focused heart shattered at the sight of the first man standing resolutely by to ensure that no one touched my things. I had assumed the worst of humanity and he had shown me the best. I was thankful that he humbly accepted my gift of the small amount of money I had in my purse before quietly resuming his way to whatever hovel in which he placed his weary head at night.

The other truck and the rope finally did the trick, and with a soul deeply touched by all that had transpired, I thanked God profusely for all the "angels" He'd sent my way that afternoon. To this day, John and I truly believe that the first might have been a *real* heavenly being. No one has ever seen him since.

In the multitude of my anxieties within me, your comforts delight my soul. Psalm 94:14. This was a verse my mentor, Doreen, had me memorize many years earlier, knowing my predisposition to worry endlessly over matters big and small. And this was the verse that flew from my heart to my head and back again on many occasions when I needed His comforting Word the most. So when there were constant rumors of a country-wide uprising, and my mind began its familiar imagining and replaying over and over of worst case scenarios, I sought "my" verse for comfort, but my fear was real, and not unreasonable, and hard to shake.

I shared my concerns, which had also become John's concerns (alarming in and of itself because very little scares my unflappable and highly competent husband) in several emails with mature Christian friends. I did not receive the sympathetic response I'd anticipated. Rather, the Lord spoke powerfully through them as with one voice they responded (though they hadn't spoken to each other about it at all) that I was called "for such a time as this" and to put my trust in God alone. He had painstakingly been training me to trust Him. Now He was asking me to trust Him even with my life. Was I willing, like Jesus, to lay down my physical life for Him? It wasn't pretty, but I once again surrendered, and immediately knew the peace that comes only from knowing the all-powerful Lord of the universe, and from knowing He loves me with an everlasting love. No weapons formed against me shall prosper!

Chapter 5

From Bad Beer to New Wine

God is the Provider.

He raises the poor from the dust and lifts the beggar from the ash heap, to set them among princes and make them inherit the throne of glory. I Samuel 2:8

We lived among people whose daily lives were a struggle to survive. We were confronted at our doorstep with clawing hunger, rampant disease coupled with lack of proper medical treatment, grossly inadequate shelter, and gaping need for someone to care. Their pain was our pain and there was no escape for any of us. I often fell into the trap of believing that I must do my best to meet every need, and of course I always fell short. I thanked God often for my husband's wisdom and discernment about how to be the best possible stewards of the support money we received from churches, friends, and family, because in spite of their huge generosity, there was never enough to go around.

I was also profoundly grateful for the ever-present guidance of the Holy Spirit. He patiently and diligently led me out of my own well-meaning but ultimately unprofitable compulsion to randomly give what I could to anyone who asked. Instead, the Lord graciously held my hand, day after day, and opened my spiritual eyes to His wondrous works for His salvation purpose and for His Kingdom glory.

One warm spring day, I was taking two American visitors through a particularly tough squatters' camp. The place reeked of human and animal excrement, and we had to be careful where we stepped. Broken glass and jagged rusty metal threatened all the bare feet of the half-dressed, ragged children who ran about largely unsupervised. My spirited interpreter was undaunted and valiantly led us through. By this time, I was becoming unfazed by the mess, and was pleased as those who knew me greeted me warmly by name.

Many men and women, stuck in the seeming hopelessness of their dreary lives, drank home-brewed alcohol made from fruit and whatever else they could appropriate. They huddled in groups of five to ten, and those who were still sober enough to pay attention to me ducked their heads in shame; others lay passed out on filthy grass mats in the heat of the afternoon.

One inebriated man, however, seemed enraged at our presence rather than embarrassed at his state, and though he was obviously old and ill, didn't seem ready yet to give in to complete despair. He drunkenly taunted us from where he sat, hunched over, on an upended broken plastic bucket. His cronies muttered unintelligibly while his two medium-sized, brownish dogs snarled menacingly in accompaniment with their owner.

The speed of events that happened next still amazes me to this day. I said a quick prayer asking for guidance, convinced my abashed interpreter to tell me exactly what our harasser was shouting, and responded to his challenge to come preach to them, against all conventional wisdom and in spite of my own timidity. The Holy Spirit simply took over and I set forth my conditions. I would share the Word of Life with them if they would restrain the dogs and refrain from interrupting.

I think they were more startled than I was at what was transpiring, and quickly agreed to comply. I am no gifted evangelist, but the Holy Spirit is, and through my surrendered lips He delivered a brilliant, concise Gospel message that day. Though the old man refused to be outwardly moved, he carefully observed as three women came forward to receive Jesus, and deliverance, and eternal life! And the angels in Heaven rejoiced.

One of those three women, Juliane, commenced to attend my weekly Bible studies very near her hut. It wasn't long before she asked for prayer. She sold home-brewed alcohol in order to feed her family, including the elderly man, her philandering husband, who had returned home after many years so that she could take care of him in his illness and old age. Juliane asked for God to show her another way to feed her family as she knew what she was doing was wrong. I prayed with her, giving her reassurances that He would help her, while masking my own lack of assurance that He would do so. Several weeks later, she ecstatically reported to me that the Lord had brought to light her way out. She explained that she had an old hand-cranked sewing machine that needed "minor" repair. If I could just help her get it fixed, she could sew for a living. My heart sank, because I had neither any idea how to help her get the machine fixed, nor the money to do so. I explained all this and told her we needed to pray together for a miracle.

God is faithful to His promises, and He showed His great love for this sincere new believer. An American friend gave the money, a repairman was found (a small miracle in itself in this rural backwater!), and the machine was made operable for this dear, faith-filled daughter of the Most High God.

∽

We often simply presented the needs to our American friends and then left it in the hands of God with awe-inspiring results. In another sewing story, a group of village women had been given the same sort of hand-cranked sewing machines as Juliane's. Some other missionaries were teaching them the finer points of creating items they could sell. This crew knew they had been given the priceless gift of a way to support their families, and they worked very, very hard from sunlight to sundown, deftly turning the crank with one hand while guiding the material with the other, all while sitting together on the ground of a wide cement veranda in front of the two-room concrete dwelling of one of the ladies.

While performing this backbreaking and finger-numbing endeavor, they sang jubilant praise songs all day long while their small children played in the dirt nearby. I delighted to hang out with them when I could, as their joy was contagious. However, I noticed as the days went by that some became a bit discouraged. When I pressed for the reason why, several challenges were revealed. One was that the older ones were struggling to see well enough to do the close work required. The other reported issue was that they wished to work even longer hours but were unable to do so because once the sun went down, they no longer had enough light. Candlelight was definitely insufficient.

We prayed together and their strong faith was infectious. I too believed God would intervene. Of course, our loving Provider answered our pleas through the generosity of donations of reading glasses and kerosene lanterns, plus a huge supply of kerosene. All I could do was laugh hilariously with them as they danced and sang and praised the Lord for His blessings.

~

During our second winter in Swaziland, I had bronchitis once again and was thankful to have a bed and warm blankets under which to snuggle and recuperate. When I ventured out, I inadvertently discovered (or more likely God revealed to me!) that our friend Philemon and his two wives and 12 children had only one blanket between them. To make matters worse, I knew they slept on the cold, hard ground. My heart breaking, I mentioned their plight to a few friends from our home church in Arizona in an email. Less than 24 hours later, money was pouring in and we were able, through shrewd shopping and the bargaining skills of my husband, to purchase 56 blankets!

I could hardly wait to distribute them as it was still very cold at night, but my wise husband exercised caution and restrained me from rushing headlong into do-gooder mode. Instead, though still overly eager, I asked the Holy Spirit to guide us to those He would have us bless in His Name.

Of course, the obvious first stop was to Philemon and his clan. Each child stepped shyly forward one by one as their father called their names, and politely received their gift. Once each one had received their treasure, the unrestrained African dancing and singing praises to God began, as we received the greater treasure, for *"It is more blessed to give than to receive"* (Acts 20:35), and oh, the joy God gave us in this enterprise!

We were met with equally enthusiastic gratitude at each stop to which God led us, until one last blanket was left. Our translator, who was helping us find the recipients, softly suggested a woman she knew of who desperately needed to know the love of Jesus. We concurred, and she directed us to a village with which we were not familiar. The sky was getting darker with nightfall and a fast-approaching storm, and my apprehension grew as we approached the conglomeration of lean-to shacks, mud huts, barking mongrel dogs, and not-so-friendly faces peering at us out of the murky shadows of lush undergrowth and bare tree branches.

Our interpreter questioned one grudging villager after another about the woman's whereabouts as my husband did his best to navigate our vehicle, weaving through the dirt between closely-built huts as inky blackness began to settle menacingly around us. Finally, we located her, and even in the grim darkness, we could see the fear and defeat in her eyes, the same look victims of unremitting violence have worldwide. She showed us her right hand, the hand she used until recently to earn a living weeding in the sugar cane fields. It was now haphazardly bandaged with blood oozing through. She explained in halting English that her boyfriend accused her of sleeping with another man and chopped all her fingers off with his machete. She was shivering in the cool night air and without hesitation we handed her the last blanket, and told her that Jesus loved her.

Of course, we were aware even before we moved to Africa that hunger is widespread. We knew it in the abstract sense that most Americans know it, and cared in the detached way that most Americans care. Once we moved to Swaziland, we saw it in the desperate eyes of mothers who starved themselves so that their children could eat, in the vacant eyes and scrawny frame of the old man who wandered aimlessly up and down the dirt road to our village, and in the slow-motion begging of the hands of children rubbing their distended bellies. I began to know it in the marrow of my bones through those Swazis I loved fiercely because of their awareness of their utter and complete dependence on God for every morsel they ate, and for their fathomless gratitude for each bite.

One practical way we could help was to hire a young mother of six to do housework for us. At the time, she was in a horribly abusive relationship, so this provided her a way out from her abuser. She was HIV+ but rarely missed a day of work in all the years she was with us, serving faithfully. We also hired a painfully thin but cocky young man who had been orphaned, along with his older brother, when he was a young boy. He came to work for us as a gardener and soon proved not only his strength as a worker, but also his innate intelligence and wit. He charmed his way right into my heart and I claimed him as my Swazi son.

Early on as the five of us (John, Jeremy and I, plus Sibongile, the housekeeper, and Phinda, the gardener/adopted son) were learning the rhythm of doing life together, we Americans were shocked to our core and given a huge wake-up call about the strong survival mode in which most Swazis live. We tried very hard to live frugally, as all eyes were on us, the white people. One day, we had handed Phinda a bag of rotten potatoes. We had carefully salvaged those tubers we could, but the rest of the foul-smelling contents were, to us, beyond redemption, and we congratulated ourselves that at least the remains would go to our compost heap. About an hour, later we were startled to hear delighted giggles as the two survival artists, Phinda and Sibongile, gleefully cut off the still-edible bites of the putrid-smelling potatoes to take home to devour.

Another jolt to my American sensibilities occurred when in my ignorance, I chose yet another unsuitable ice breaker for one of my Bible study groups. With a smile, I asked that day's question, "What is your favorite food?" and then gave my answer as it always helped them to open up if I went first. I confessed my weakness to chocolate only to get a silent but undeniable reaction I didn't quite understand. As they one by one gave their forthright answers of "meat," I realized my blunder. To them, meat was a luxury ("Any kind!" was their response when I questioned them further), only to be had at weddings and funerals. As women, they only got the bits deemed inedible by the men who, by cultural rights, got the choicer parts. I guess it was by God's grace that these women loved me unconditionally despite my mistakes; that, and they knew that I loved them passionately and unconditionally back.

~

There are many organizations that provide food in southern Africa with varying rates of integrity and success, from local churches to international aid organizations. It is neither my place nor the purpose of this book to judge or report on these matters. However, one organization has earned a huge place of respect in our hearts, and that is "Feed My Starving Children." Hundreds and hundreds of children DO receive daily sustenance from this wonderful ministry at feeding sites known as care points. A large part of our own ministry was to the faithful, hardworking women from the communities who served as cooks for the local children at these local care points out of love for God and for their people, receiving no pay other than enough food for their families each month.

We also served with a local church which oversaw these care points. The pastor of this church was a Portuguese woman with a faith and a heart as big as Africa itself. In addition to caring for the children, her heart also bled for the elderly, and each year she provided a feast for the old folks from the surrounding villages. She delighted in giving them several kinds of meat, vegetables, the ever-present "pap" or corn meal mush, rice, and even dessert. Those of us preparing and serving the food turned a blind eye to the majority of grannies and grandpas who surreptitiously brought cloth or plastic bags to slip food into when their shrunken bellies, unaccustomed to such bounty, wouldn't hold any more. The year ice cream was served, much quiet laughter ensued among the servers when the melted, goopy cream was dumped right on top of spinach, beef and gravy. That was the last, and only, year ice cream was served.

~

Many of us did what we could, as best as we could. My friend Lisa came to visit one year with a suitcase filled to the brim with specially-designed tuberculosis masks donated by a medical professional acquaintance of hers. When we presented them to the nurses at the hospital, tears of joy flowed from their eyes; prior to this gift, they'd been caring for wards of tuberculosis patients without any sort of protection. As we did with every gift that passed through our hands, we emphatically gave credit and honor to the ultimate Gift Giver, and proclaimed that Jesus Christ died and rose again. *"For God so loved the world that He gave His only begotten Son, that whoever believes in Him should not perish but have eternal life."* John 3:16

Of course, no thinking Christian could witness such widespread suffering and not have many questions for God. I am no theologian, though I do understand suffering has to do with sin entering the world. Even through my questioning, my faith that God is completely good while completely sovereign has remained a tension about which I have a peace. I have far too often witnessed God's miraculous love to doubt it for a moment.

I grew up in the desert, and one of my fondest childhood memories is of my daddy trying to grow a few vegetables in the hard, dry desert dirt in our backyard. I knew no better, and was always enchanted when a few scraggly green shoots would poke through, even though nothing ever grew to become truly edible. So imagine my elation in Swaziland where the soil is a rich, dark red, and our brilliant Phinda practiced the gardening techniques every Swazi child learns in school.

In chapter 28 of Deuteronomy, God promises blessings to those who obey Him. Verse 8 says, *"The LORD will command the blessing on you in your storehouses and in all to which you set your hand, and He will bless you in the land which the LORD your God is giving you."* Oh, how He blessed us in abundance in Swaziland, to overflowing. We had a bounty of mangoes, bananas, oranges, lemons, papayas, mulberries, strawberries, potatoes, tomatoes, zucchini, many varieties of chili, green peppers, green onions, red onions, yellow onions, coriander, rosemary, maize, garlic, yellow corn, cucumbers, lettuce, spinach, broccoli, cauliflower, pumpkin, carrots, beets, okra, green beans, peanuts, and more. By not only sustaining us but by giving us plenty to share with many others, the Sustainer of all life demonstrated the wealth of His mercy and compassion to His people.

When we left the United States with untainted and optimistic hope of truly making a difference, one of our big goals was to help build a children's home for a few of the millions of children in southern Africa left as orphans from the AIDS epidemic. By this time, AIDS had ceased to grab the world headlines, but at least there was now greater awareness, in spite of the subsequent greater apathy towards our suffering African brothers and sisters.

The plight of the children became personal to me when I visited Swaziland for the first time. I was chatting with a woman who was doing her best to help her community by cooking donated food for hundreds of children each day, almost all of them orphaned and vulnerable children. She looked at me straight in the eye and told me that there were many children sleeping in the tall fields of grass at night. She reported that she was able to keep an eye on them during the day and protect them as best as she could, but that at nighttime they were left vulnerable to the evils of human predators. I cried out to God in heartbreak and desperation. He cares for the orphans of this world, and He answered. Due to the extreme generosity of several dear friends as well as the vision of our local pastor friend and the donation of land by the local chief, we were able to build the home.

───

God allowed us to be a part of His charitable acts in so many ways. He also kept us humble since the acts of kindness were so obviously His doing and not our own. As well, He graced us with people in our lives whose lights shone so brightly, and whose acts of generosity so far outshone our own.

One of these people was a crippled, disfigured old granny, who had very little herself and often ran out of food. But her standard custom was to be on the lookout for hungry children as they passed by her home on their way from school. If one seemed to be especially in need that day, the child was invited in for some bread or eggs or porridge. And if a neighbor came asking for help, the neighbor was invited in to take as much as they wanted, even if it meant that her shelf became bare.

Two women, Christina and Linah, whom I fondly referred to as the "twins" though they were not related at all by birth, epitomized for me the ultimate of selfless giving. They first told me their story during one of our Bible study sharing times. They always sat together, rode to church together, and lived in shacks side by side, so it was obvious that they were very close, but I had no idea why until their story unraveled, in the detailed, rambling fashion in which African stories are told.

Christina had first fled to Swaziland many years earlier, leaving behind an unfaithful husband as well as starvation in the war-torn neighboring country of Mozambique. As has been true throughout history, and is true in every people group, migrant outsiders are usually at best resented and at worst persecuted. But Linah knew Jesus, and she had His compassion for the alien and the widow firmly embedded in her heart and soul. When she met Christina and learned of her desperate circumstances, Linah immediately proposed to her husband that they allow Christina to stay with them in their little one-room abode. God moves in the hearts of kings and husbands, and miraculously he agreed. They shared all they had with Christina, a complete stranger and foreigner to their land.

To this day, I question whether I could ever be that selfless. It keeps me humble and pressing on to attain such heights of the Father's love for the downtrodden of this earth.

Chapter 6

"Mhlengi is broken! Mhlengi is broken!"

God is the Miracle Worker.

...Who does great things, and unsearchable, marvelous things without number. Job 5:9

Life is a miracle. A baby is a miracle, and each breath and each sunrise after that birth is a miracle. All of God's creation is a miracle, but we often fail to recognize the miraculous in our daily lives. In Africa, however, sometimes those miracles became unmistakably apparent!

My friend Lisa and her daughter Molly were visiting. One pleasant evening, the five of us were resting after a demanding and exciting day of ministry together when suddenly there was a loud banging on our back door. All the windows were open so we had no trouble hearing our neighbor shouting, "Mhlengi is broken, Mhlengi is broken!" The man's panicked voice was loud and clear, but the message was not. We knew who Mhlengi was; he was the darling three-year-old son of our housekeeper, who lived about one hundred yards away. What we were having trouble comprehending was that this child was "broken." After a few quick probing questions, things became clearer. The messenger was doing his best, in his frantic, broken English, to let us know that Mhlengi had broken his right arm, between the elbow and shoulder, when he'd fallen from a tree.

As the only white people and the only ones with a car, the politely unspoken hope was that we would help, and of course we obliged. We all trooped over to properly assess the situation, and Lisa, being less squeamish than I, felt the arm where the bone was clearly not at the proper angle. It was frighteningly bent in a way which a child's arm should never be bent. We prayed--hard.

Sweet Mhlengi had already learned what all Swazi children learn: life is hard and it does no good to cry about it, so it is best just to endure silently. Even the rough drive over poorly maintained dirt roads elicited only hushed groans from the back seat where his equally stoic mother gently held him.

It took about twenty minutes for us to reach the surprisingly clean and efficient rural clinic, and Molly kept Mhlengi occupied reading a child's book to him. Though the book, written in English, was completely incomprehensible to him, he obviously relished the unaccustomed attention and comfort being lavished on him. Meanwhile, John helped Lisa with the payment process, and we all prayed some more until the attendant came to fetch us. My son Jeremy had opted to stay home since we couldn't all fit in the car, but there were still six of us, and the kind night nurse allowed us all to troop back to the examination room with her.

She confirmed that the arm was indeed broken, but cautioned that x-rays should still be taken. She gently fashioned a sling for Mhlengi and told us to go to another clinic (much farther away) in the morning, as this clinic had neither an x-ray machine nor plaster available for the cast, and the other clinic would be closed by the time we could get there. It was very late by this time so we had no choice but to return home. And we prayed some more before we all fell into exhausted slumber.

Swazi mornings start early, usually before the sunrise. We all gathered for the hour-long journey...and prayed. We immediately noticed that Mhlengi was laughing and joyful; the bouncing boy was quite different from the subdued patient of the evening before. Lisa and I later confided to each other that we suspected a miracle, and we soon learned it to be true. The doctor examined both the x-ray and Mhlengi's arm, and pronounced him healed! Thank You, Jesus!

I have nowhere near the wisdom to know for certain why there seem to be so many more miraculous healings in Africa than in the US, but if overwhelming anecdotal evidence is to be counted, it seems that this is true. For sure, we had the joy of witnessing our fair share!

Once or twice every year we had the honor of serving alongside medical mission teams who would come from the US to do what they could for the thousands of locals who could otherwise not access medical care. Each day the dedicated volunteer team of doctors, nurses, and lay people saw hundreds of Swazis who waited patiently for their turn for basic examinations, diagnoses, and whatever treatment could be provided on site. Our role as part of the local host church was always to ask each and every patient if they had a relationship with Jesus Christ, and also to pray with them for whatever their needs were. It was a beautiful opportunity to lead many to the Lord, and though the days were long, there is absolutely no joy that can compare to welcoming new brothers and sisters into the Kingdom family!

Of course, many also wanted prayers for healing, and we duly complied. It was late one afternoon, and our energy was waning in the confined heat of the cramped quarters. I am embarrassed to admit it, but to be honest, my prayers had become somewhat rote when a young girl and her uncle approached us. Each patient carried with them the paperwork from their examination, which gave us their diagnoses and any care instructions. But we didn't need the document to tell us that her eyes were crossed. Her uncle informed us that she had been that way since birth, and subsequently also suffered blurry vision and frequent headaches.

Ncamsile, my dear interpreter, and I dutifully mouthed the appropriate words for healing, but my heart wasn't in it. I'd seen so much suffering all day and despaired that any of my feeble prayers would ever really amount to anything. Nevertheless, I heeded the prompting of the quiet voice of the Holy Spirit to cover the girl's eyes with my sweaty hand as we were reciting our petition.

When we finished, I dropped my tired hand to my lap...and did a double take. Right before us, those crossed eyes moved slowly into their proper places. The whole process took maybe ten seconds, but my mind was much slower to accept what I had just witnessed. I wondered if my own fatigued eyes were betraying me, and rubbed them with my fists. Sure enough, her eyes looked perfectly normal now. I turned to Ncamsile and whispered, "Did you see what I just saw?!" She appeared as dazed as I was as she smilingly nodded, "Yes."

Uncle conferred with the girl who shyly reported that she could now see clearly for the first time in her life! All good news from God is made to be shared, so we took our charge to the medical team which was just finishing for the day, looking as bedraggled as we'd felt before the awe-inspiring phenomenon occurred. Needless to say, everyone became animated with amazement, and the miraculously healed child looked on with wonder as everyone exuberantly rejoiced! *"...Not by might nor by power, but by my Spirit..."* Zechariah 4:6.

On another similar occasion, my husband prayed for an elderly gentleman and watched, astounded, as the scales literally fell off his eyes. Diagnosis: cataracts. Healer: Jesus!

Then there was the time an evangelistic team came and prayed for a four-year-old child who had never walked. We observed no immediate change, but the preacher was convinced that "something" had happened, though I was quite skeptical. (*"Lord, I believe; help my unbelief!"* Mark 9:24). The next time we visited that community, the same boy was running to greet us!

~

It is true that children hold a special place in God's heart. Unfortunately, they are not always as valued by their parents or other caregivers. Predominantly, households in rural Swaziland consisted of either single mothers or grandmothers who were often so overextended just trying to survive that they had little left over with which to properly care for and nurture their own children, much less the children of family members who had died whom they were now also raising. The majority of children we interacted with were simply left to their own devices.

As you can imagine, many of these precious children came to harm. The children's wards at hospitals were full of kids with snake bites, broken bones, and burns. Especially burns. Most homes had no electricity, so fire was the only source of heat for warmth and cooking. Fires were frequently left as unattended as the children were.

As I was visiting with some of the women in one of my Bible study groups, a sad tale poured out. The day before, one of the women in their village had locked her seven-year-old son inside their mud hut, ostensibly to keep him "safe" while she got drunk enough to pass out outside in the dirt. Somehow he tipped over a lit candle and flames quickly engulfed him. He survived but was covered in charred skin and was taken by ambulance to the hospital, about a ninety-minute drive away. As always, the tacit expectation was that I would pay for the medical care, but this time I simply did not have the funds. I did all I could do, and led them in prayer for the situation.

I have no idea who finally paid the hospital fees (a pittance by American standards but still way beyond the means of the impoverished villagers) but I do know Who healed the young boy. He does bear the scars of his ordeal over much of his body, but no less than a week later he was back running and playing with his friends. I admonished him that God obviously had big plans for his life, and that the scars were to remind him of what God had done for him! Praise the Lord!

The most precious healing of all to me personally was that of my beloved Ncamsile. I do not have the medical background to explain why, except that it has something to do with malnourishment, but many Swazis have strokes (and many other premature medical problems) at an early age. I learned this abruptly when Ncamsile, then thirty-four years old, had a massive stroke and was hospitalized and not expected to live. In fact, the three other stroke victims, all women, in the beds next to and across from hers in the dismal ward, all died while she was there.

As she tells the story, she became angry at Satan and began praying in earnest for the Lord to heal her. And He did, expeditiously and completely! And my dear Swazi sister has testified more times than I can count of her own personal miracle, and encouraged many a frightened stroke victim and their despondent families that there is hope because Jesus cares!

~

Jesus doesn't limit His power to healing. He also performs innumerable other wonders on our behalf and for His glory! Remember the biblical stories of the loaves and fishes? I experienced a modern-day version!

It thrilled me each year to hold large "women's day" events. All the surrounding communities were invited to these gala affairs, and our local pastor generously paid to have many eager women transported to the church for the occasions. Each event had a biblical theme, and I gave a corresponding message. As well, we played whatever relevant games or activities I could conjure from my God-given imagination, using whatever donations were on hand (as our budget was quite tight), sent by American friends who were always generous contributors of a myriad of goods, often intended for children but gleefully transformed by me into games for "my" ladies. It never ceased to tickle me to orchestrate amusements for them as these normally somber, downtrodden women suddenly converted to giggling females for a few precious worry-free hours.

Of course, food was the real draw, not my fertile imagination nor lovingly constructed biblical lessons, nor even the gay social atmosphere. I couldn't provide much of what in my American mind constituted a feast, but for them, polony (the southern African version of bologna) and processed cheese (often all we could get at the store) sandwiches, fresh fruit, chips, and cake were a wondrous change from their normal routine and bland diets.

As time went on, I became more and more adept at throwing these parties for a culture so vastly different from that in which I was raised, though we laughed together over my many social blunders in the process. The first event was almost a disaster.

It was Christmastime and I so desperately wanted to do something special for the women. With the pastor's permission,

I made the announcement from the pulpit about the upcoming party. I carefully instructed them how to sign up, explaining clearly and repeatedly that I needed to know exact numbers so that adequate transportation, goodies, and food would be available. To my dismay, only about twenty women signed up, though some of the assistant pastors reassured me that I could expect twice that many.

As The Day approached, I diligently counted and recounted each of the donated goodies to ensure there would be more than enough. I carefully planned the food with the same goal in mind, yet not wanting to waste the hard-earned money of our supporters either. I had pretty little Scripture cards (though few could read--but hey, they were free and pretty and I knew they would be treasured), three hard candies, and delicate Christmas ornaments for each participant.

In typical Swazi fashion, the guests arrived over an hour late, and my volunteer worship team, who also graciously doubled as my helpers for the party, was already worn out from helping me set up, and then from singing boisterous praise songs until the last busload had been delivered. As each group arrived, my emotions alternately leapt like the graceful and plentiful impalas, then plummeted as quickly as the setting blood-red African sun.

At first, I was thankful that anyone at all showed up, because I'd had no idea of what to expect. Then I was ecstatic as more than I'd expected began walking through the double glass doors. Finally, my heart began to pound harder than any impala being hunted by a hungry lion as I lost count at more than double the attendees for which I'd prepared.

As the jubilant ladies, dressed in their finest attire of their least threadbare mismatched blouses and skirts (which somehow only African women can wear and still look beautiful and stylish!), joined in the gleeful singing and dancing unto the Lord, my panic was full-blown. I fled to the relative quiet of the church foyer where I could be alone to re-strategize what I felt was an impending catastrophic situation. Unbeknownst to me, dear Abraham was also there, and I poured out my woe to him while he silently and respectfully listened. Then, in his simple, faith-filled way, he smiled and reminded me, "Loaves and fishes, loaves and fishes." He promised to pray as somehow I felt unable at that point in time, and I rushed back in to begin the scheduled activities.

The ladies were so excited to have their very own party and were suitably receptive to my simple Christmas message. However, I realized too late that the frivolous activities I'd so earnestly crafted for the occasion were grossly inappropriate and ludicrous to them.

We all muddled through and they tried so very hard to gamely please me, though they clearly had no idea what was expected from them or why they were performing such nonsensical tasks as decorating miniature Christmas trees. In retrospect I comprehended that they'd never had materials to decorate anything in their lives, and that all of their daily physical energy went into basic survival tasks.

I began praying in earnest after instructing my helpers to cut very small portions of the cake, hoping but absolutely not believing that somehow miraculously there would be enough to go around. My first inkling that Someone other than my ill-equipped self was in charge of the day and loved the ladies infinitely more than I did was when there was enough cake and punch left over for every single one of the eighty-two attendees to have a second helping, and for us even to share with the bus drivers and dear Abraham.

The day was saved when the food was served, and the jovial atmosphere once again became a lively din. Christmas here in Africa is in the summer time, and we were all hot inside the concrete structure with no air-conditioning or even a fan, but it didn't matter. These precious women felt special, maybe for the first time in their lives, as women are mostly regarded in their culture as insignificant, powerless, and virtually slaves.

The time came for the end of the festivities, and I announced that the buses had arrived to take them back to their crude homes. But I had one more parting shot at blessing them. I had been so excited to hand them each their meager presents. With a sinking heart, I remembered that I had counted and recounted these, and I knew beyond a shadow of a doubt that forty gifts were not enough for eighty-two women.

Too late, my helpers had begun passing the goodies out as I had instructed them to do at the beginning of the day. All I could do is to join in and pray for wisdom on what to do once they ran out. The women were all lined up as they one by one clapped and squealed upon receiving their treasures. I silently counted and held my breath as forty-one, forty-two, forty-three...fifty-five, fifty-six...sixty-seven, sixty-eight women passed and the large bowl continued to supply, never becoming empty until the very last, eighty-second woman unknowingly received a true miracle of God's multiplication. There were exactly enough! That day was by far the most special Christmas present I'd ever received--God revealed Himself to me, in no uncertain terms, as the Gift-Giver of miracles who loves us with an abundant, overflowing love.

As I ardently taught over and over, the greatest miracle of all was what Jesus accomplished for us with His death on the cross and resurrection to eternal life. Through this greatest act of sacrificial love, all our sins are forgiven, and we can have eternal life with Him! This is something we as Christians can take for granted after years of hearing the same stories and reading the same verses. May we never become callous or cease to be grateful.

We from affluent countries also take for granted owning a Bible, or two or ten different versions, as well as assuming the ability to read them. Not so for our Swazi brothers and sisters. Another of our greatest joys was placing donated Bibles into hungry, outstretched brown hands. We knew the majority of the recipients were illiterate, but also that in most families, at least one child had been to school at least through the early grades, so we fervently hoped that God's life-giving Word would be read aloud by families in their homes.

God always out-gives anything we have to offer, and this giving of Bibles was no exception. Just as I was becoming (sigh, yet again) a bit proud of the work we were doing, He humbled me to the core.

As Ncamsile and I were having another fulfilling day of distributing Bibles, she stopped me from my usual speech about making sure the Bible was read and not relegated to the dust pile. She asked the woman to whom we were handing the Bible to tell her story in her own words. Ncamsile knew Esther, and knew what had already transpired. Long before I came on the scene, God was there. Esther trusted Him as only someone destitute can trust, and begged Him for a Bible. He provided through a traveling preacher. Next, she pleaded, as only those not made cynical by having an excess of material goods and false intellect can plead, to be able to read her Bible. You see, Esther had never attended school in her life, and could not read a single word, yet she knew in her heart that what was between the covers of her priceless book would sustain and bless her for a lifetime. Her faith was rewarded. Ncamsile was a witness that long ago day when Esther opened up her Bible…and began to read, clearly and precisely, out of Psalms. She hasn't stopped reading since, and showed me the proof in her now-tattered, stained and well-worn Bible that was missing many pages and literally coming apart at the seams. God's gift to me that day was to shatter every cynical precept I'd ever learned by teaching me irrevocably that He is the God of impossibilities!

Chapter 7

A Teddy Bear's Gift

God is the Comforter.

>...*To comfort all who mourn*... Isaiah 61:2

Wonderful surprises came with our visitors, who often brought one and a half suitcases full of delightfully diverse donated items. This limited them to only one half of a suitcase for their own belongings, which they then usually left as well, flying back home to the US with literally only the clothes on their back and whatever souvenirs they could manage to stow in their carry-on baggage. Our guests were invariably eager to divest their bags of the plethora of wealth hoarded over months as they prepared for their trip here. And I likewise invariably cried upon seeing the bountiful treasures. I process things slowly, and it was often months before each precious item found the person I believed to be the recipient for whom the Holy Spirit intended it.

One morning, in preparation for our team's monthly excursion to minister at the hospital, I was sifting through the three closet shelves which stored donations until the proper homes were revealed. Due to a longer period of time than usual between visitors, the shelves were uncharacteristically bare, but tucked back in one dimly lit corner I found a lone, gently-used wee teddy bear. Disregarding practicalities, as children are always in wards together and it simply would not do to give one a gift and not all the others, I heeded instead that still small voice whispering to me that today I would find this little stuffed bear's new heir.

Upon arrival at the hospital, we started, as had become our routine, in the women's wing. After obtaining permission to visit the patients, we began our usual rounds, sharing the Gospel in each ward and then praying individually with each receptive and grateful sufferer. We encountered the usual cases of tuberculosis, diabetic amputees, snake bite victims, and assorted other maladies including pneumonia, strokes, and influenza, almost always compounded by weakened immune systems due to AIDS. Many, in their dire conditions, were eager to receive Jesus as Savior.

We had reached the last ward, and the very last bed in the wing. The occupant was a woman, somewhat plump and very young. She was obviously in terrible pain, though in stoic Swazi fashion was doing her best to suppress how excruciating it truly was. We could see her blood oozing out onto the sheet in the area of her stomach, and she fearfully and tearfully poured out her horrific story, taking off the blanket and exposing her completely-bandaged midsection which was still seeping frightfully bright red blood. She had been attacked by several young men as she was walking alone to her rural home. They each raped her in turn, and when she tried to defend herself, they laughed and hacked away at her tummy with their bush knives. They'd left her for dead, but a friend found her and managed to obtain transportation for her to the hospital. Her husband had refused to have anything to do with her, blaming her for the crime, and she had no living relatives. She was shamed, terrified, hurting, and so horribly alone.

I stayed with her as long as I could while the others went on ahead to the men's and then the children's wings. I listened and I prayed and I read her Bible to her, and yet still I felt there was more I needed to do. I couldn't quite grasp what that might be until I remembered the small stuffed bear in my bag. But surely the little animal was meant to comfort a child, not a full-grown adult woman who had seen the very worst abuse life had to offer? "Yes, her," whispered the Comforter, and yet I dallied just a bit longer, not wanting to offend her with such a childish thing, as though something so insignificant could ease her physical and emotional anguish. "Yes, her," He exhorted once again, and I obeyed before the doubts in my mind could resume.

Oh, the deluge of tears that were released as she clutched the little toy bear to her chest and thanked me profusely and repeatedly. I left knowing she was in good hands. God knows; He always knows. I am convinced that every tear of ours that falls is accompanied by twice as many of His. And He knows just how to bring consolation to each pain-filled heart to draw it to His own.

Any culture in which women are deprived of individual rights also tends to have vulnerable women and children who are abused at the whim of those who have the power, namely men. Often the men are from their own families where women and children are virtual slaves. As a professional counselor in the US, I often worked with clients who needed to heal from such abuse, as no society in this fallen world is immune to such evil. Yet never had I encountered so many victims of physical and sexual abuse as I did in Swaziland. The majority of women seemed to have silently suffered as children and continue to suffer as adults.

Counseling sessions were much more informal in rural Africa as there really is no siSwati word for "counselor," nor even any real comprehension of that profession or role by the majority of uneducated Swazis. Often the counsel took place in group settings as the need was revealed during Bible study sessions. Sometimes I would meet with individuals referred to me by the pastor. Often my professional "first world" counseling skills were grossly inappropriate and insufficient, which led me to rely completely on the counsel of the Lord.

The Bible often mentions Jesus being "moved by compassion." Oh, how I felt compassion for these women who kept going, kept loving, and kept living in spite of such debilitating, dehumanizing attacks in their lives. Perhaps it was this very compassion of Jesus flowing through me - though I felt so helpless to help them heal - that restored their dignity and gave them strength not only to carry on, but to do so praising God and serving Him with joy.

After two such heartrending sessions, I was the recipient of words of comfort from the very ones I wished to console. One elderly survivor simply placed her gnarled hand on my breast. (Swazi women are much freer with touch than we Americans are, and this was a common gesture I'd learned to accept as normal.) She began patting me and saying, "You are my mother; you are my mother." I understood immediately that she was telling me I'd nurtured her as a caring mother would, and I thanked God for allowing me the privilege of sharing His love. *"As one whom his mother comforts, so I will comfort you..."* Isaiah 66:13

The other occasion that touched me deeply was a statement from a middle-aged woman who had been part of one of my Bible study groups for several years. She said simply, "Kay, you console our hearts." *"Blessed be the God and Father of our Lord Jesus Christ, the Father of mercies and God of all comfort, who comforts us in all our tribulation, that we may be able to comfort those who are in any trouble, with the comfort with which we ourselves are comforted by God.* 2 Corinthians 1:3-4.

Perhaps my most poignant memories of all are of the countless funerals in which I was honored to participate. Death in Swaziland is an all too common occurrence. It rarely happens behind sterile hospital doors but rather in the home. It does not honor age; children and young adults are often the ones who are buried. One year, as I was desperately trying to comprehend so much loss, I morbidly counted the number of deaths of those I knew, improbably trying in my own feeble way to dignify each one and to say, "You will not be forgotten." The number that year was eighty-three.

With so much death, the Swazis cope with stoicism. There is little overt comfort given to family members who are grieving a loss because those who would normally comfort are still buckling under their own bereavement. Every man, woman, and child have wounded hearts, with no time to heal before the next fatal blow occurs. Conceivably this is why their funerals are so impassioned and heartrending. Each burial service is a time for true communal grief, where not only the deceased being honored is mourned, but also it seems that death itself is lamented, as the sorrow for losing so many loved ones comes pouring out in a deluge of anguish. It is both terrifying and beautiful.

Traditionally, Swazi funerals take place after an all-night vigil. Untold times I would leave our home in the heavy, haunting stillness of the African bush at night, the hushed silence broken only by the occasional cry of a wild animal. As I traveled through the unrelenting darkness, I was always relieved to pick up my pre-arranged passengers further on as they piled somberly into my car so we could travel together, often for an hour or more, to whichever rural homestead held the lifeless body and still-numb family members of that occasion.

The singing, always the singing. Oh, how Swazis can sing! Melancholy tunes tinged with Swazi hope-filled words of heaven softly filled the vehicle as I pushed on through the pitch-black night. Once we'd arrived, the anguished crooning from the homestead reached across the shadows to greet us, and our songs and theirs gently met in the middle as our sorrowful hearts likewise joined together in soft but perfect harmony.

One by one we were escorted to view the body one last time, approaching on our knees, as was customary. Then we'd take our place with the others on grass mats and rough blankets side by side for the duration of the night.

As the sounds of impending daybreak began to penetrate, the summons was given by the patriarch or presiding official for the body to be moved to the burial site, where the hole had already been dug by the male members of the family. I was once told by a young Swazi gentleman that Swazi men dig approximately one grave site a month, and I have no reason to doubt his estimate. The whole assembly would walk one by one or in pairs to the grave site, usually about a half a mile, where we would once again sit on mats and blankets, or just on rock or a softer patch of the ground. The speeches would begin, as one by one family members, pastors, and dignitaries shared stories and consolation.

As the only white person, I was always accorded the status of dignitary and often asked to speak. I was embarrassed by the distinction, yet always grateful for the opportunity to share the gospel of hope at a time when hearts were the most open and attuned to things of eternal significance.

As the body was lowered into the ground, and the inevitable "thunk, thunk" of shovelfuls of dirt were placed on the coffin, the wailing of female family members began in earnest. The rest of our gathering accompanied them with songs of heaven just as the sun would rise over the hillside.

Our last goodbye gesture, per tradition as well as out of practicality, was for us women to each traipse off to find a medium-sized stone to place around and on the grave, ostensibly an attempt to ward off wild animals from digging up the body. Exhausted sisters, mothers, aunts, and female cousins were then expected to feed the multitudes of mourners, but those of us who had travelled far were given takeaway containers so we could be on our way, almost gasping to escape the clawing vestiges of death, and grateful to breathe in God-given life again as we resumed our daily routines. And I prayed, oh, how I prayed, that somehow our feeble gesture of just being there brought some comfort, and most of all that those in grief would reach for the consoling arms of the God of all comfort.

May it never be that I make it seem as though we did all the giving and the Swazis all the receiving. On the contrary, there is no doubt in my mind that we received far more from them than we could ever repay. Therefore, I see fit to conclude this chapter sharing about the love poured out to us, touching us deeply.

God so completely transforms hearts that those who suffer the greatest are ironically the ones who are able to be the most comfort to others, completely eradicating what the enemy intends for harm and instead metamorphosing pain into agape love. Our precious Swazi brothers and sisters blessed us time and again when, in the midst of their much-greater suffering, they came to our aid in times of need.

Two such occasions were when we lost beloved pets. Swazis do keep dogs, but those canines are not pampered and cherished in the way we Americans have the luxury of pampering and cherishing our pets. Swazi dogs are sometimes companions, but usually simply tolerated around the home to deal with vermin and to chase off human intruders as well. Those dogs survive on scraps and whatever they can hunt down around the homestead.

Our Swazi friends' willingness to accept what to them was our eccentric behavior towards our animals (that we treated as part of our family) is a testament to their love for us, as well as an amazing willingness to accept other ways of life. Oh, how they laughed to see our small dachshund mix, Barnabas, on the bed. They were astounded that even our giant Neapolitan Mastiff, Boaz, and Boerboel, Baby Ruth, were allowed on the sofas.

Sadly, both Boaz and Baby Ruth died while still very young, within a year of each other. We were much too far away from any veterinarian to get help, and had to watch helplessly as each passed in our living room. Both times I cried disconsolately while our dear neighbor men did the only thing they knew to do, and what they do so well. They dug graves for our "babies." They didn't laugh or mock, but simply joined us in our grief and helped John bury our pets, and then, when exhausted he came in to grieve with me, they decorated the graves beautifully, as though royalty had been buried there. Flowers were planted on top, rocks were carefully chosen and placed, and in our time of sorrow, our precious friends brought us peace, comfort and love.

Chapter 8

A Supper of Almonds, Mints, and Beef Jerky

God is the creative Creator.

For with God, nothing will be impossible. Luke 1:37

I thrive as a classical musician, not because of any natural creativity on my part, but rather because classical music is very mathematical and I relish the structure. Through sheer hard work I mastered the rules and became a proficient instrumentalist and music teacher, if not an inspired one. However, my few early ventures in high school into the world of musical improvisation failed abysmally! While my soul yearns to be free to fly, the brutal truth is that I work best with clear guidelines, proper procedures, and formal order.

My Creator, apparently, decided this particular human creation needed some more molding and shaping, and He knocked me completely off balance by moving me to Swaziland where such structure was lacking. I could only regain any equilibrium by relying entirely, completely on His genius as I faced circumstances requiring great innovation, ingenuity, and inventiveness. Through my extremely adaptable Swazi sisters and brothers, I learned the fine art of reshaping old familiar ways to fit new circumstances. Through my Potter's firm hands, I became fashioned more and more into His creative likeness.

∽

The sacrament of communion, in addition to being a commandment, is also an act I personally hold dear. It doesn't matter to me if it is done with great pomp and formality as it is in some churches, or if it is sweet and informal at a family's kitchen table. I'm as comfortable with grape juice as I am with wine, and with stale crackers as with soft sweet bread. I revere the communal time to remember the broken and bleeding sacrifice of my Savior and to rejoice in the Unity He accomplished on the cross. It was imperative to me that communion be a vital part of our Bible study groups' fellowship.

Accordingly, after my first couple of months teaching a Bible study to our initial group of women, I felt it was time for us to observe the Lord's Supper together. There are no convenient stores in which to purchase usefully-labeled communion crackers in rural Swaziland, and our choices at the supermarket in the nearest town were few: brown or white, sliced or unsliced, and a whole loaf or a half a loaf (for those who could not afford the whole). I chose a whole brown loaf. Also, most Swazis call a cheap sugary flavored mix (similar to the packaged products I did not like even as a kid) "juice," but I was determined to spend the extra money to obtain real, one hundred percent juice for the occasion, obsessed with any excuse to get even an ounce of nutrients into their nutrition-starved bodies.

After borrowing communion cups from the church, I navigated my way over the potholes, through the bush, and past the ever-present sugar cane fields to my destination. Upon my arrival the ladies began preparing to come, as the only way they knew it was time for our weekly Bible study was when they saw my red car weaving its way up the dirt road leading to their aggregation of huts. While they washed as best they could from small rubber tubs filled with water from the canal, and changed into their best clothes, I proudly spread my own grass mat, the first of many of these lovely handcrafted items gifted to me over the years, on top of the hard-packed dirt under a lovely old shade tree where we met in the early days.

I cannot remember what I taught on that day, except to emphasize the horrible beauty of Jesus' ultimate gift. I then read the appropriate verses I'd chosen and asked a few of the twenty-five or so women present to begin distributing the tiny cups and chunks from the loaf of unsliced bread while we sang an exquisite Swazi song about Cavalry.

It was only then that I truly noticed the ever-present children. We had no cheerfully decorated and safe church nursery for them to be placed away from the adults, and I always vaguely delighted that the wee ones always joined their mamas in hearing God's Word. They were always so well-behaved and quiet, some leaning against their mamas or other women, some in laps, and some playing quietly with rocks in the dirt nearby, that I really only noticed them peripherally. My passion and my mission were to the women, with the vision of them passing what I taught on to the village children. But this day was different. I'd brought food, and suddenly their hungry, pleading eyes were on the sacramental provisions.

These children were too young to even begin to grasp the theological concepts of redemption and restoration. They simply watched with empty bellies and meager hope as the elements were passed to their elders. With a quick prayer, I did what I believed Jesus would have done. I asked permission from the grateful women to give the rest of the food to the children, with the simple words to the little ones of "uJesu uyakuthanda." "Jesus loves you."

Without exception, these times of celebrating communion together were special for all of us. I never wanted it to become routine so we only practiced the rite several times each year, and each time was truly precious.

Hunger was ever-present, and I was wise enough to try to conceal the juice, bread, and cups until after I had taught the lesson. I knew otherwise their concentration would be completely and understandably on the physical sustenance available rather than the spiritual. However, as time passed, they became wise to my wiles and began recognizing the telltale signs of a bulging plastic bag. Once that bag appeared with me, I knew I had to follow through!

Imagine my chagrin when we began in the usual manner and I reached into the bag to find the cups and juice and... gasp, I'd forgotten the bread! What to do? In quick succession:

quick prayer, confessed my mistake, and asked a teenage girl to run to the little village store in the hopes they had a loaf of bread. Disastrously, it was almost sundown and the proprietor had already closed and locked the shop, making her way home before the dangers of nightfall. Just when I felt completely forsaken and doomed, I was given a flash of divine inspiration.

There were two young American women, short-term missionaries, with us that day. I remembered I had a few lint-covered mints at the bottom of my purse but knew there were definitely not enough to go around to the multitude. The loaves and fishes miracle had already happened once and I was not so sure it would happen again. I had already cautioned the Americans, as I do with all visitors from lands of abundance, to conceal any items of food they might have brought with them that they did not wish to share. So I whispered a frantic plea, "Do you have ANY food in your backpacks?" After a rapid check and consultation, they whispered back that they had a few pieces of beef jerky, and a small bag of roasted almonds.

As I have already confessed, I tend to be obsessive about many things, including obeying orders and doing things properly. Yet I knew, with my entire heart, that that day we had God's blessing to honor the Lord with the spirit rather than the letter of the law. We thanked Him for His spilled blood by taking the juice, and for His broken body by carefully dividing and partaking of tiny bits of jerky, a single almond for some, and a couple of mints for others. And I know He was pleased.

Another way God increased my creativity was by guiding me in developing culturally appropriate Bible study lessons for the ladies. In the U.S. I'd thoroughly enjoyed watching Beth Moore videos with women friends in our comfortable homes where we took turns hosting Bible studies. I relished times with my close friends as we chose from a wealth of literature designed for individual and group studies of God's Word, with challenging discussion questions at the end of each chapter full of details about the Greek or Hebrew definitions of key words. I did not recognize then how much our affluent culture was a part of all those studies - in the presentation of material, in the probing life-application questions, and in the format itself.

There was no question in Swaziland that showing a video of beautifully coiffed and garbed white women, sitting in a plush living room in front of an ornate fireplace, and teaching wonderful truths in English to an educated and well-fed audience was not only ridiculous, but impossible. My Swazi sisters lived where there was no electricity, most were uneducated, and few spoke English. Written references to movies, husbands with jobs, or frilly coffee drinks would have been meaningless to them.

It was my joy to spend hours and days pouring over the stories of women in the Bible, and yes, researching the Greek and Hebrew and commentaries as any Bible teacher should, who recognizes the high standard to which God holds us. But more than that, He began helping me to see these stories through the lens of my Swazi sisters. So much of the Bible was written by and to an agrarian people who also used lamps for light, and depended solely on God's grace to water their seeds and to multiply their livestock. I'd venture to say that there are far more references in the Bible to handling crops than to our more modernized, westernized sermonizing about balancing pocketbooks by not overspending on shopping sprees. Even the concept of a man marrying more than one woman, which was so inconceivable to my American sensibilities, was perfectly normal to them. Oh, how they related to the anguish of those women of the Bible who had to share a husband.

I learned so much from those times of experiencing God's Word come alive in new ways. As a result of my own delight in discovery, I became quite the animated and creative teacher. Whereas in the U.S., I would have certainly been voted the least likely to ever achieve poise speaking in front of a group (as I was rather previously a staunch member of the sweaty-palms-and-knees-knocking-together club), teaching became my absolute joy. He equipped me to become adept at reading my audience and responding in the moment accordingly, or spontaneously sharing a pertinent story, or comfortably switching gears entirely in a session as the Holy Spirit led. Created in His image, I became creative, and I loved it!

Sometimes even my own newly discovered, God-given creativity wasn't enough, and the Holy Spirit Himself had to intervene. Such was the case in the Moms in Prayer International prayer group I led each week. As we interceded for each other's children and their schools, it was imperative that we understand each other so we could agree in our prayers for them. With God, all things are possible, and even though in the early days

I understood very little siSwati, and they understood even less of my heavily accented English, when we gathered to *"pour out [our] heart[s] like water before the face of the Lord"* (Lamentations 2:19), He miraculously created a way for us to hear and understand each other. This was confirmed on those occasions when we were blessed with a human interpreter joining us. I cannot explain it to this day; like all true creative miracles, it just was.

As I mentioned, Swazis are highly adaptable. Prior to being immersed in a group of people who had to regularly make something out of nothing as a means of survival, I was completely unable to think out of the proverbial box, but oh, the tricks they taught me! Children routinely amazed us with their creative use of anything they could get their hands on to play with. Discarded plastic bread bags bound together with pieces of frayed string tied together became a soccer ball. Scraps of rusty metal became a makeshift toy car. Any variety of games could be played in the red dirt using only pebbles.

Several instances of adaptability still bring a grin to my face and laughter in my heart. One of those was the case of the roof rats. In our roof. Several friends in Phoenix were already familiar with the scurrying pitter patter of little rodents above their heads, but we had to move all the way to Africa for the experience. Once we realized what all the furry commotion was, John managed to track down an alleged pest control company of sorts. The voice on the other end of the phone (thankfully

Refiner's Fire

in order that day!) promised to send someone out "tomorrow," which we knew might mean the next day, but could also be the next week, or the next. We resigned ourselves to an uneasy wait.

So of course we were suitably grateful when two men did come out within a matter of days, and eagerly expected quick results after all our patient endurance. Oh, would we ever learn? First, the matter was discussed interminably (okay, maybe for about 30 minutes). Next, we were asked if we had a ladder the pair could borrow as their boss had dropped them off and they had no tools. After inspection was made through the dingy crawl space, they promised to return...the next day.

When they did come back, they were again summarily deposited and without the proper equipment. They did have rat poison, but could they use a few of our tomatoes in which to deposit the rat poison? Lacking the proper dispensary, they knew tricks! Sure enough, within a few days the scampering ceased and the stench of decaying flesh began...and we had to find creative ways to disguise the odor until God-knows-what took care of the remains!

~

Food was serious business in Swaziland, not only as a means to fill hungry bellies, but also as a necessary supplement for the medication taken by the many with HIV/AIDS to boost their immune systems, or for the antibiotics used to fight tuberculosis. Niceties like sparkling clean dishes or sanitary eating conditions were simply not as important as desperate attempts to satisfy growling tummies. There were the horrifying stories circulated of people eating dirt just to fill the void, and I was told by many that as children, they were simply taught to go to bed early as a way to temporarily forget the hunger pains.

These were the sad stories, but I collected many first-hand funny ones as well. At the church, we had several refrigerators, not only to keep food cold for special events, but also just as a place to store food where the ants and other critters couldn't reach it. Like so many things, I learned this trick the hard way when I neglected the refrigerator trick for the beautiful cakes prepared at our pastor's home. When my helpers and I rushed back to the kitchen to begin serving the ladies, I was dismayed to find the entire cake tops swarming with ants.

A side note: If you have never been to Africa, you don't truly know insects. I am originally from Texas where everything is bigger, but I'm telling you, ants and roaches and any number of other pests are bigger in Africa, and just MORE than in Texas, and that's a hard thing for a Texan to admit! Pesticides did not make a dent. Geckos on the walls of our home become our treasured friends, as did the toads croaking outside our windows during the rainy seasons, because they became our best allies in eliminating at least a tiny portion of the epidemic of creepy crawlies that was our constant lot.

Back to the infested cakes. While I stood shaking my helpless little blond head in consternation, my practical Swazi helper immediately began brushing the offensive vermin off the cake. In spite of my protests of the cake no longer being edible, she just as promptly ignored me, cut the cake, and served it with the admonition not to waste a crumb of food, ever.

This same indomitable sister also taught me another invaluable maneuver. At another church event, someone had inadvertently left a huge pot of grated beets for a moment, before they were to be cooked to serve to the voracious waiting crowd. My friend and I discovered the nightmarish spectacle of ants covering the entire massive heap in the pan. I think I have mentioned how resourceful my Swazi friends are? My accomplice chuckled as she placed the entire mess on the old gas stove, and commanded me to quit squealing and watch. As the pot began to heat up, I stood transfixed as the ants began to make an increasingly hasty exit up the sides of the pan. The exodus accelerated as the heat intensified, and first a few of the ablest escapees made it to the top of the scorching pan, and then the rest of the horde, only to fall to their sizzling death in the fire below! With a conspiratorial wink, my friend victoriously signaled that the problem was solved, and we served the delicious beets to one and all. And, yes, I ate some!

Mother's Day is celebrated in rural Swaziland, if and when, and only if and when someone who has access to a calendar remembers. Being the "calendar queen," I made it my job to remind many a husband as well as our pastoral staff about honoring all the mommies. Unfortunately, the message didn't always reach all its intended targets, and one year, the dear man serving as pastor at a daughter church either didn't get the reminder or forgot that morning. When I smilingly asked him later in the week how the annual celebration went at his church, he looked suitably chagrined. But like the ingenious Swazi he was, he simply honored the mothers the following week and no one else was the wiser!

～

A final note in this chapter that my fellow musicians will appreciate. You will remember that at the beginning, I told you that in spite of being a teacher of music for many years, I was always completely incompetent in improvisation. Fast forward to my eagerness to play on the church worship team in my new African church home, and the complete necessity of playing entirely without notes in front of my face, or often without even a chord chart, or plan of a key. Ack! God equips those He calls. Slowly but surely, I overcame my fears and allowed Him to overwhelm me instead, and I worshiped him with my eyes closed and my fingers availing themselves of His inspiration alone to create music.

Chapter 9

A Man Named "Wonderful"

God Saves.

Then fear came upon all, and they glorified God, saying, "A great prophet has risen up among us!' and 'God has visited His people!" Luke 7:16

I briefly mentioned before that I am not gifted as an evangelist. Like many, I used to use this as an excuse to avoid the uncomfortable. I believe God had had enough of this subterfuge I had adopted to evade obeying His mandate to all Christians everywhere to share the Good News of salvation through Jesus Christ. Once He plopped me down in Swaziland where people were truly perishing before our very eyes for lack of His Word, I became passionate, if still not very gifted, about leading people to the Lord.

A dear friend had given us the "Jesus" film in siSwati before we left the U.S., but of course, finding the opportunity and the venue was quite a challenge when most did not even have electricity, much less television screens. The only movie theater in the whole country was built several years after we moved to Swaziland, and it was a good ninety-minute drive from where we lived. Finally, however, God opened the door for this wonderful movie about the life and ministry of Jesus to be shown at the local church during one of the women's day events I hosted.

I had to scale down my fanciful American notions of providing popcorn and soda for the ladies as the pastor was understandably not too keen on having sticky floors littered with popcorn hulls for her church service the following morning. Of course, no one but I had any idea that the experience was lacking in anything! Most of these precious ones had never seen a movie before in their lives.

As excited as I was to provide them their very first cinematic experience, I had no way of predicting how they would respond. For those of us who have been exposed from birth to moving pictures, it is not a startling experience. Our brains have learned, for the most part, to translate what is transpiring before our eyes as not "real life," per se, but simply actors playing the parts. Most of my Swazi gals had at least heard of movies, and had a basic idea of what they were about to see, but the phenomenon proved far more intense for them than any of us could have imagined. Seeing the life of Jesus portrayed right before them, on a very large screen, was all too realistic to them.

We were a double act that day, the ladies fully captivated by the movie, and I, standing in the back, fully captivated and enchanted with their engrossment and very physical responses to the scenes being played out before them. At first, they were utterly still and quiet (a rarity in that crowd!), spellbound and transfixed. Then, as the events unfolded, they laughed, they stood up and cheered, and the "oohs and ahhs" were seemingly inhaled and exhaled with every breath. They were truly on the edge of their seats, and I began to fear what would happen when the "hard" parts came. The emotional impact for them was visceral, and all too visible to me. They flinched, they fell on the floor, and they wept.

My natural reaction was to want to comfort them and to remind them, after it was all over, that it was "only a movie." The ever-present Holy Spirit reminded me that the story was very, very real, and to allow Him to have His way in their hearts. Many repented that day and accepted Jesus as their Savior. I fervently pleaded with the Holy Spirit to help me teach them to follow Him as Lord.

I had several wonderful role models in the art of evangelism, including our local pastor friend, who never missed an opportunity to share about her beloved Redeemer. Complete strangers, including the police who pulled her over for accidentally speeding, the grocery store clerk, or the ladies selling vegetables by the roadside were all asked the same question, "Do you know for certain where you'll go when you die?" And off she went, telling about her wonderful Savior named Jesus!

Then there was our friend Philemon, whom I have mentioned before. I have to tell you that he was one of the most powerful, sincere evangelists I have ever witnessed. He and I left *before* sunrise for church on Sundays to meet the prayer team for intercession *before* the worship team rehearsed *before* the service started. That is a lot of "befores" and should clue you in to how lengthy Sunday mornings were! However, services started long *before* we ever reached the house of God.

I never drove anywhere in Swaziland alone. It would have been horribly rude since we had one of the few cars around. So even in the wee hours of the morning, many were standing on the side of the road hoping, to spot us passing by so they could catch a ride. I left our house alone but usually arrived at church dispersing a carload, feeling like one of the circus clowns I'd seen as a child who were all piled into a tiny Volkswagen Bug, and gleefully jumped out one by one to the delight of the astounded audience.

Sometimes, though, our passengers were on their way somewhere else, and I felt safe enough to pick up women passengers who were perfect strangers, or if Philemon was already on board, men as well. Once they were captive inside the vehicle, Philemon wasted no time. I could understand enough siSwati soon enough to understand that he was rapidly and fervently giving his own testimony before we had to drop them off at their destinations. He talked, I prayed, the Holy Spirit convicted!

Philemon was not at his usual spot one Sunday morning, and I missed his silly antics of dancing and jumping on the roadside to make sure this absentminded driver didn't pass him by. It was virtually impossible to miss him, even for someone as perpetually preoccupied as I am, as he stood well over my tall husband's six-foot, one-inch height. And once he began his weekly shenanigans, he conveyed the impression of a tattered scarecrow puppet with his raggedly-clothed, scrawny limbs jerking this way and that, with far too much animation for even my still sleep-fogged brain to miss.

I was appalled the next week when he explained that he had been in jail. I was also shocked at his absolute joy in the retelling of the story. Repeatedly, I had to ask him to explain more clearly how he'd landed in jail in the first place, because that was not the piece of the story he wanted to relay. While I was concerned for our friend's welfare, he was concerned about giving God all the glory for his ordeal.

Apparently, he had benevolently jumped into the middle of a brawl in an effort to separate two neighbors who were viciously fighting each other. When the police were called by others to intervene, Philemon was unceremoniously thrown into handcuffs and incarcerated with the other two. As the altercation happened on a Friday evening, he was held until Monday morning when the story could be sorted out, at which time he was released to reluctantly return home.

It is not that he did not want to be with his family again, away from the rats and the stench of his cell. Rather, he was reluctant because, in the fashion of the Apostle Paul, he viewed the walls of his confinement as just another opportunity to praise his God. In just two days, Philemon led seventeen desperate men to Jesus, and Jesus set the captives free.

My own experiences with the police were not so heroic, though I do have some fond memories. Once after another six-hour Sunday marathon of providing transportation, intercessory prayer, worship team rehearsal, and a two-hour church service, John and I were headed home in our respective vehicles. He'd picked up my Bible at church for me while I was assisting elderly passengers getting in my car for a ride to their homes. I was exhausted by the time I'd gently helped each frail commuter out of the car and into their huts, and was gratefully approaching the turnoff to the dirt road leading to our house.

My heart sank when I saw the police officer flagging John down. I knew that neither of us was breaking any laws. Police stops were common in Swaziland and often the officers only wanted to check to make sure things like our brake lights and turn indicators were in proper working condition. I was just so tired and eager to be home, and knew that this stop could delay things. I also knew my husband would chat with the officers, who were usually quite friendly, and interested in our US drivers' licenses. I waited as patiently as I could, knowing my turn to be inspected was next.

The man in uniform finally approached my window and curiously asked what I was doing in Swaziland. I explained that I was a missionary, along with my husband, who was the man he'd just spoken with in the car ahead of me. He got a mischievous smirk on his face and asked, if I were truly a missionary, where my Bible was. I could only hope he would believe me when I explained that my Bible was in John's car! After that, I made sure I had my Bible with me at all times!

On another occasion I was driving home alone after teaching a Bible study in a nearby village. I was approaching the same turn leading to our house when a different officer pulled me over. I chuckled to myself realizing that this time I not only had my English version Bible, but also six Bibles in siSwati as there were a few left over from when Ncamsile and I had been distributing them that afternoon. Sure enough, he asked me what I was doing in Swaziland and I replied once again that I was a missionary.

Though it was a different officer than the time before, I recognized a similar smirk come over his face. He began to badger me, in a rather mocking tone, asserting that he'd "tried Christianity," but once he'd heard it preached that a man should only have one wife, he'd never gone back to church. He then challenged me to show him where it said such in the Bible. For a moment, my ugly pride surged up and I wanted to point out multiple passages to him, but that still small voice restrained me. I knew this was neither the time to satisfy my ego with a display of my working knowledge of the Holy Scriptures, nor to attempt to engage him with any sort of overt evangelism.

Instead, I delightedly handed him one of the Bibles next to me on the front seat, and encouraged him to research the Word for himself. I obviously momentarily stunned him with my response, and he mumbled a hasty "thank you" before his smug self-confidence resurfaced. Then he cockily asked if I would give him a few more Bibles for his mates, gesturing to the other policemen leaning against their cruiser a few feet away. I knew better than to refuse and said a quick prayer that at least someone in each man's family would truly receive these gifts for what they were--God's living and active Word, the daily Bread they so desperately needed and which was so freely given. I may never know this side of heaven if my pompous harasser ever even opened the Holy Book of life given him that day, an opportunity orchestrated by the Giver of life Himself. All I could do was pray that he did, knowing that my gracious Savior would flood him with His mercy if this officer took just the first baby step.

~

God relentlessly pursues the lost, and opens so many doors for us to be His vessels for His purposes, if we will but avail ourselves and be ready when He opens doors. This was the case with my friend Lisa, who had prayerfully prepared for months ahead of time for her brief visit from the US to come alongside us in ministry.

Lisa and her vivacious teenage daughter, Molly, were thus accompanying us during our monthly visit to the hospital. It was a pleasure to behold not only the way their kindness and genuine concern for each patient touched many that day, but also the way the stories of the patients struck Lisa's and Molly's hearts. One young mother's tale in particular had the profound effect of completely arousing Lisa's compassionate nature. The Swazi mother was in her late teens and had just delivered her first baby, a darling little girl. The little fledgling family was utterly alone and destitute, and had no way to even pay the hospital fees so that they could be released to go home. Lisa innocently inquired how much the fees might be, imagining something akin to the exorbitant medical bills with which we are all-too-familiar in the United States.

While this exchange of information was transpiring, I realized that two different things were being communicated, but had no way to intervene before it was too late. For Lisa, she was just showing sympathy and interest in her direct American way of conversing. On the other hand, the young mother was Swazi, and familiar with a subtler form of interchange. It was all too clear to my more practiced eyes that what she was hearing was that Lisa was offering to pay the hospital bill. As quickly as I could, I pulled Lisa aside and explained the expectations she had inadvertently caused. We both panicked together.

We decided to follow through with Lisa's promise to go to the administration desk to get a direct quote of the cost, and off we traipsed with our interpreters, the equally bemused Ncamsile and Jane. Our anxiety mounted with the ever-slow process of getting any sort of information in the unhurried Swazi society. Finally, the cheerful attendant came with the bill, also obviously assuming that the rich American people were going to pay, because that is how Americans are viewed in Swaziland. No matter how much we protested to the contrary, most believed that all Americans are not only extremely wealthy (and in comparison to them, we are) but also lavishly benevolent.

A helpful nurse had meanwhile jumped on board and had assisted the young mother to the administration building to be checked out. With great trepidation I peered over Lisa's shoulder at the financial statement. I knew it would be far less than Lisa expected (health care in Swaziland is amazingly inexpensive), though of course still higher than many can afford. Yet I also felt embarrassed with the pressure she was under to pay. Much to her relief, the bill was less than $100, and much to my relief, she was able and willing to pay. In fact, she was ecstatic! With uncharacteristic speed, the transaction was taken care of and the jubilant young mother hugged us all over and over, repeatedly thanking us with tears in her eyes.

Yet our team all tacitly knew there was so much more in store for our new friend. We proclaimed how much Jesus loved her and how He made all this possible. We asked her if she knew Him as her Lord and Savior, and she replied that she knew of Him but had never been a believer, until that moment. Prior to that day, Ncamsile and Jane had been too shy to lead someone to the Lord, but I knew that it was time, and gently prodded them to pray with her, and they did, and we welcomed her as our new sister into the family of God.

We were five women filled to the brim with exceeding joy, and did what most women typically do in such circumstances - we wept copious tears! Dear John had been ministering elsewhere all the while and knew nothing of our victorious saga. The poor man happened to round the corner right at that moment and encountered his wife, guests, interpreters, and a perfect stranger garbed in a hospital gown all hugging and sobbing. In a manly fashion, he calmly extrapolated the story from us to ascertain the reason for our apparent female hysteria. Even my composed husband, upon hearing of God's grace in that moment, rejoiced with us, albeit in a more outwardly dignified manner.

Startling in every way was my discovery of one of the realities at the hospital where we ministered. I was no stranger to death, having been present when a friend died of cancer as well as caring for my own father in our Arizona home until he passed with us by his bedside. Yet I was not prepared for the way hospital deaths were handled in this place. Sadly, the facility lacked a lot of the modern day medical equipment I'd always taken for granted, including machines used to monitor the heartbeat, oxygen levels, and so on.

Therefore, when a person was perceived to have died, the body was not immediately whisked away. Rather, a standard cloth room divider shielded the other seven residents in the ward from viewing the body, though with the beds closely packed side by side, four adjacent to one wall and four adjacent to the other in the small rooms, there was really no escaping the harsh reality.

I learned this firsthand when a woman was thought to have passed while we were praying with others in the ward. The sisters (Roman Catholic nurses) were summoned and, in a flurry of activity, did whatever it was they were supposed to do, and the screen was hurriedly put in place. I assumed only that they were concealing a live patient for some sort of treatment, but was perplexed because seclusion was a luxury not afforded there. When I asked my team what the privacy screen was all about, they nonchalantly told me the woman was presumed dead. They were equally puzzled at my line of questioning because this was a standard procedure with which they were grimly all too familiar.

I was finally able to ascertain that the body would be left for one to two hours to make sure the woman was truly dead since there was no scientific way to be certain. I found this all very strange and unsettling, and felt great sympathy for the remaining bed-bound patients who simply had to endure this macabre situation. It seemed I was the only one who seemed at all bothered, though there were cursory murmurs of commiseration that a fellow sufferer seemed to be out of her misery. After a while, I became more accustomed to this practice, though it always left me with an unsettled feeling.

Complacency was never a state in which I was able to linger long in Swaziland. One warm, muggy day, we were making our rounds in the wards, which were ventilated only from the mostly intact windows which were flung open wide. The peeling paint, water-stained ceilings, and universal hospital bouquet of bleach, body odor and urine no longer bothered me as much; however, in this place where medication shortages prevented even enough for pain relief, the suffering still shook me to the core every time.

This particular day, I joined in the sympathetic murmuring when a privacy screen was erected around a bed nearby, and went about my business of comforting the woman in the bed in front of me. We stayed in each ward from fifteen minutes to over an hour sometimes, depending on the receptivity and need for our services. This was one of the longer times, and perhaps thirty minutes after the screen was put in place, everyone in the room heard a rustling sort of noise coming from the hidden bed, and we could see motion through the thin cotton divider! The sisters came and whisked the curtain back to find the seemingly resurrected woman sitting straight up and very much alive. Though I was probably the most surprised, I was not the only one cheering in that previously cheerless room that day!

With such close proximity to death a common occurrence in the hospital, those we visited were ripe for the good news of everlasting life in Christ Jesus. While the work was emotionally and physically draining, there were so many moments of elation and joy when another human being was snatched from eternal suffering and saved by the gracious blood of Jesus.

Many of the patients at the hospital had tuberculosis, an epidemic in Swaziland as it is an opportunistic disease affecting those whose immune systems are already compromised by HIV. There was a separate TB ward of sorts, but the door opening into the common hallway was often left ajar, I presumed for ventilation on the many hot days. On my first visit to Swaziland, I gratefully accepted one of the two available masks offered to the four of us visiting. My dear husband bravely declined so that our friend could have the other one. Once we moved to Swaziland and visited the hospital on a regular basis, I learned just how precious and scarce those masks were, and decided to simply trust the Lord to protect me, as often they were not available at all. Those on my team who were HIV+ wisely declined to enter but the rest of us always went in to share His love.

One day, John came upon a middle-aged man who was enduring not only the agonies of TB but also other ailments. He spoke decent English, and seemed to enjoy John's jovial company. Swazi culture is more genteel than that in which I grew up, and it is imperative to spend time getting to know a person for a bit before diving into deeper matters. So after the customary back and forth niceties were observed, it was already apparent to us that this man was likely not a Christian. My beloved patiently explained salvation by faith through grace to him and then led the perishing but eagerly willing man in a prayer of salvation. It was only after this always miraculous new birth took place that John realized we'd missed an obvious social nicety and did not even know the man's name. Our new brother's name was "Wonderful!" Yes! Wonderful day, wonderful grace, wonderful Savior!

Chapter 10

And the Walls Came Tumbling Down

God is Victor.

The sting of death is sin, and the strength of sin is the law. But thanks be to God, who gives us the victory through our Lord Jesus Christ. 1 Corinthians 15:56-57

I am not a screamer, per se, but given the proper incentive, I am able to let out a respectable shriek. Such was the case one glorious spring day in October. The jacaranda trees were blooming, the bougainvillea and African lilies exuded their exquisite scent, and I had a rare day at home to catch up on a myriad of chores and projects at a leisurely pace.

John was out and I had spent the morning trying to conquer the long list of ministry and personal correspondence, longingly peering through my windows with their sheer curtains gently wafting in and out, reminding me that there was a gentle breeze to temper the warm sunshine just outside. When I'd tamed but not quite completed the task at hand, I decided to take a break and stroll around a bit outside. After a short walk, I was feeling refreshed and turned toward home, ready to return to my computer while the Internet was still working.

As I approached our veranda, my brain struggled to comprehend what my eyes perceived. The veranda was my favorite place in the house and I spent many pleasant hours there at our cheap little café table with its rickety chairs, reading my Bible, having candlelit meals with my husband, or daily eating my usual breakfast of fresh fruit, granola, and plain non-fat yogurt. The view was stunning year round, with the rugged hills in the near distance, green sugar cane all around, and our lovely flower gardens and tropical trees spread everywhere. There was a short wall all around the veranda that was maybe 2 feet tall, supporting the screen that reached to the roof and mercifully kept the insect hordes mostly out.

The supporting wall was painted a light yellowish-green shade, but no matter how many times I rubbed my eyes, the normal color did not materialize that day. At first I thought that someone had decided to paint the entire surface with mud, as I had once proudly done to our backyard walls as a small child, and for which I was soundly chastised. The whole wall was a sort of dark reddish-brown hue, and as I got closer my eyes also reported that the maroon mass was moving. To my horror, I finally perceived that the entire thing was completely covered in large ants so thick that they were crawling on top of one another. Some that could not gain a foothold were falling off at my feet. Thus the shriek.

Our dear Phinda was working in the vegetable garden on the other side of the house, but came gallantly at a gallop when he heard my unmistakable female cry of distress. Being the practical born-and-bred African man that he was, he calmly asked me for the insecticide and went to work. His businesslike response had a soothing effect on me, and soon I was gleefully joining in the fray, maniacally cackling and stomping on as many of the intruding army who tried to escape as I could. It took us about a half an hour, but we finally won the battle over the enemy, and praised God for the victory.

Phinda and I delighted in telling and retelling our story of the wall of ants we conquered, and had many laughs afterwards recalling our efforts that day. Just so, I delight in telling stories of God's victory over the real enemy. What Satan intends for harm, God uses for good. I've witnessed it time after time.

So often when I was training women in prayer warfare and teaching them how to form groups under the banner of Moms in Prayer International (MIPI), it seemed the enemy tried to sabotage our efforts. There was the aforementioned incident with the cobra for example, and many other equally daunting situations.

Such was the case when about twenty-five women were gathered under a huge tree. My interpreter, Fikile, was doing her best to interpret the finer points of praising God, confessing our sins, giving thanks, and interceding, all from the expansive English language into the more limited siSwati. All were intently listening and the hot afternoon was relatively peaceful until suddenly we heard a piercing feminine screech accompanied by the lower pitched shouting of a discernibly angry man. I know I was not the only one who flinched involuntarily as we heard the indisputable sounds of a domestic squabble.

My immediate concern was for the woman's safety, but I knew that I could put myself in very real danger by intervening, especially in this particularly violent village where even members of the police force were often reluctant to enter. However, it quickly became apparent by the sound of things that she was probably the aggressor and in no immediate danger. Just as I asked the petrified Fikile to interpret what the fuss was all about, hurled rocks began flying over the high grass wall, the only thing separating us from the combatants.

My heart was pounding and I knew I had to take charge quickly. Fikile wanted to run to the shelter of my car, and the village women were thoroughly distracted and distressed. I quickly prayed asking for help, and before I knew it, I was giving orders in an uncharacteristically commanding voice. I told Fikile to sit still and trust God. Then I instructed my still-trembling interpreter to direct the other women to sit down and to listen. Fikile might have been reluctant, but she has a voice like an opera singer and her orders pierced through the drunken shouts still assaulting us from the other side of the fence. My voice is soft, but through my much louder interpreter, and with the authority of the Lord, we called upon the women to pray for the brawling couple next door.

This was something that never would have worked in the US. But African women pray loudly, and all at once. There is courage in anonymity, and as one they began shouting their prayers for peace and reconciliation and God only knows what else. It worked. The couple became silent. We resumed our training session with new zeal having just witnessed the power of prayer to a victorious God! Best of all, months later, the embattled wife gave her life to the Lord!

⁓

Tragedy is often the impetus for unity. One of our Bible study groups was located in a village comprised of not only Swazis, but also quite a few migrants from the neighboring country of Mozambique. Many of the Mozambicans had fled to Swaziland decades earlier during the brutal civil war in their home country. The Mozambique border was very close to us, and many had settled in this village, having been given small plots of the meager land by the local chief on which to build their huts.

Given the fallen nature of man, strife between the tribes was inevitable and ugly. Our Bible study group was an uneasy mix of both Mozambicans and Swazis, and squabbling frequently broke out among them, though they tried to hide it from me. No matter how often I gave them Scripture exhorting us to be kind, to welcome the sojourner, to walk in love towards each other, petty jealousies kept the group in almost continuous disharmony.

For two years my interpreter for that group, Clarah, and I dismayed. It seemed nothing would ever change, but she and I persevered in prayers of faith and hope. Satan was having a field day in that community in more ways than one. Crime was high, and drug abuse was rampant, especially among the young adults. I arrived on my usual Tuesday afternoon to find an unusually subdued group. In rambling Swazi style, the story came out, and eventually with Clarah's help, I was able to piece together a myriad of details to comprehend the horrific tale they were imparting. The weekend prior to our meeting one young man had hanged himself from a tree. Another young man, son of one of our members, had tried to follow suit, but miraculously his rope broke, and he was still alive.

The ladies were clearly still reeling from the gruesome events and looking to me for guidance. Once again I was way out of my depth. My professional expertise in grief counseling was no match for the raw and primitive emotions of this down-trodden and distressed gathering. Their fear for their children and others in their community was palpable and they were feeling defeated. I was honest; I told them I did not have the answers but that God did. I asked them all to close their eyes and to pray with me, in the usual Swazi style all at once and out loud, asking the Lord to help us.

Inspiration came like a flash. The Holy Spirit did not speak to me in an audible voice, but He might as well have. This horrible tragedy, and these feelings of utter helplessness and defeat, would be the catalyst to draw this diverse and divided group together in unity. God would bring beauty from ashes. And He showed me clearly how to proceed.

I began sharing about MIPI with the ladies, and asked if they would like to form a prayer group in their community. They immediately caught the vision, and hope rose in that bitterly winter-cold concrete schoolroom like a warm blanket of Swazi sunshine. Outside, we could hear the sounds of the body of the young suicide victim being brought back to the family's home for burial. Inside, we spoke of praising God to defeat Satan, and of confessing our own sins of bitterness and unforgiveness, and of thanking God in all circumstances, and of interceding for our children using Scripture. We marched together to the little graveyard behind the village to attend the funeral and console the grieving, and afterwards we marched back to our meeting place as one.

From that day forward, these former adversaries banded together in prayer for their children and the children in their community. Friday became their chosen spiritual warfare day, and God was victorious in their hearts.

One of the women in this same group was a feisty middle-aged woman named Roaster who was known not only to hold a grudge, but also to be quite outspoken about it. Thankfully she also loved the Lord very much, and began taking His teachings about forgiveness to heart. As God trains us in each new thing, He also allows us to be tested as any good teacher would.

Roaster's test was severe. She loved to eat chicken, and of course, getting to eat it for her wasn't as simple as going through a fast food drive-through window and placing her order. No, chicken was a rarity, reserved only for special occasions, for this mother of two adult daughters and their three offspring, all living under one roof. Roaster was wealthier than most in that she actually owned two chickens which were laying eggs for the family, and which would provide meat as well once their laying days were past.

Then came the night of the chicken raid. Roaster woke up to discover her precious duo missing. The police were called (as I said, food, and meat in particular, was a serious business in Swaziland!) and the culprit was soon discovered. The thief was an emaciated young neighbor in his early twenties who shamefully confessed his crime, the chicken bones still before him on the ground where he'd been eating his spoils. He knew there was no excuse, but he'd recently lost his job and was hungry.

He was unceremoniously dragged to Roaster's door to repeat the confession. What happened next, from the way Roaster's older daughter relayed the story later, seemed to shock Roaster almost as much as it did the officers, who well knew both her and her reputation for vengeance. Roaster had been washed by the blood of Jesus and sanctified by His Word, and she immediately told the astounded group gathered in her yard that she forgave the culprit.

I have no idea what happened to the pardoned chicken thief and any observers after that, but I have to believe that the events that transpired, and the transformation of an angry woman to a giver of mercy, had to have an impact in their own lives. Grace triumphed, once again, over sin and death.

Grace also triumphed over pain and sickness. I will never forget standing with the hospital team by the bed of a thirty-something-year-old woman. She spoke fluent English and was obviously well-educated and less impoverished than those we normally encountered on our rounds. All these observations were possible only later on though, because even before we turned from the patient in the bed beside her, we could hear her moans of agony. We came face to face soon enough with her contorted body and misery-filled eyes. She was able to gaspingly inform us that they did not know what was wrong with her, and many on our team believed she had been cursed. Curses were a huge part of Swazi culture; regardless of your own belief system, to the Swazis they were very real and very powerful.

Thankfully, our team also believed in the greater power of entreaty to the all-powerful, conquering Savior. We prayed. The woman stopped writhing and groaning, and began smiling. We began smiling. Together we all began laughing and praising God. Her story tumbled out of her still-grinning lips. She used to go to church, but somewhere along the way she lost her faith. She was certain that without the physical torment from which she had just been miraculously healed, she never would have believed again in the Father's great love for her. Now she knew that even though she'd taken her eyes off of the Lord, He'd never taken His eyes off of her. He defeated the foe who tried to snatch her from His hand. Jesus won.

It was impossible not to notice her. Her small limbs jerked seemingly of their own accord, and her child's body was contorted at an impossible angle. Her calloused knees were scabbed and scarred from their constant friction with the ground on which she was forced to crawl since she could not walk. I guiltily hurried past her grotesque form and into the tiny village market to make my purchase.

A few days later, my conscience intervened and I awkwardly handed her a few trinkets I'd selected for her from the donations shelf: a tiny rag doll and a cheap cross ornament. The jerky movements increased, and squeals of delight as well as unintelligible sounds I assumed to be attempts at speech in siSwati issued from her twisted lips. My discomfort at her unusual appearance began to give way to enchantment observing her simple joy. I asked my interpreter to find out more about the young girl, whom I presumed to be about six years old. Since most Swazis are small in stature, and the children in particular often look younger than their actual age due to malnourishment, I was only mildly surprised to learn that she was ten. I was still embarrassed at the age-inappropriate gifts I had chosen, but also knew that they were possibly the only toys she'd ever owned, and probably the only gifts she'd ever been given.

We learned that the sweet, helpful woman who managed the market was her mother, and that her father left when she was an infant. A medical missionary friend I'd contacted confirmed what the ancient paperwork, scrupulously preserved by mom Jane, showed to be her diagnosis—cerebral palsy. The school system was not equipped to handle "differently-abled" children, and "Sister," as she insisted we call her, was one of several in that village who would never get a formal education due to their special challenges.

In my newfound zeal to somehow make a difference in Sister's life, I made another huge blunder early on. Our community Bible study group was beginning to gel, and the ladies were excited with my suggestion that we do a prayer walk around the village. I requested that our first stop be at the market to pray for Sister, and they readily agreed. There must have been twelve or fifteen of us who descended on the unsuspecting child that day, and we terrified her. I noticed the fear in her eyes and cowering mannerisms first as the others had their eyes closed, all praying in their usual cacophonous manner. I had to shout several times for them to stop and to back away, and I silently grieved that the actions I'd instigated might have seriously traumatized her, though her mother reassured me later that she was fine.

I invited Jane to come to our Bible studies, and when she was unjustly fired from her job because of unsubstantiated accusations, God turned her anguish into a blessing since now she could join our group. The ladies all pitched in to carry Sister to our spot under the big tree, and mother and daughter quickly became regular fixtures.

Jane and I soon became good friends. She had grown up in a close-knit Christian family and loved the Lord. She worked tirelessly at multiple jobs and ran several small businesses to provide for her children. A tiny woman, she was also incredibly strong and able to carry huge loads of firewood on her head, or transport Sister on her back even when Sister grew to outweigh her in later years. And the mealie bread (similar to our American cornbread) she cooked and sold, but freely shared with us, was absolutely delicious! My new friend was highly intelligent and well-educated but in a country with such high unemployment she was unable to get more than "piece work"—menial day labor-type jobs such as weeding the cane fields by hand. Yet she never complained and was one of the most loving, giving people I have ever known. I admired so many things about her, but most of all I admired her devotion to Sister.

Oh, how Sister loved it when it was time for "church," as she called our little weekly gathering. Her favorite part of all was praise and worship time, and her raucous, discordant, and wholly discernible-only-to-God songs brought us all so much joy. She was loud and praised her Lord with an abandon, and we all adored her.

Soon Jane began bringing Sister on the bus that provided transportation to the "real" church. The pastor welcomed her and insisted Jane place her right in front of the sanctuary where there was soft carpet for her rather than the cement which comprised most of the flooring where the congregation sat. As I was on the worship team, John and I also sat up front. While I was on stage, I could watch with delight as she sang along with all her might, arms flailing in praise, right and left hand doing their best to meet together to join in with the clapping throng. Though the electronically amplified sound system drowned out her strident voice, I know the Lord heard beautiful sounds from her radiant face.

As I exited the stage each week she anticipated my hug, but it was John's attention she craved most. He and she soon developed their own little routine. When she became bored with the sermon, she would reach out to him with her foot, striving with all her might to exert enough control over her own wriggly body to touch his. She became quite adept at connecting with his size 15 shoe, and they played the most adorable game of "footsie" I have ever seen.

Year after year, Sister watched as the children she grew up with were awarded graduation certificates from the little preschool at the care point. Due to her special circumstances, it was deemed unnecessary by the teacher to bestow the honor on Sister since she returned, year after year, with children increasingly younger than she. My heart broke when I found out, so John and I devised a plan. We let the ladies know that we were going to surprise Sister with her very own graduation ceremony. Jane kept the secret from her daughter while craftily managing to prepare Sister for the special occasion without her knowing. Therefore, when we arrived, Sister was thoroughly washed and scrubbed, but confused as to why all her "friends" were arriving all at once on the little veranda in front of the family's one-room apartment. I had the honor of performing our little ceremony, and I began by announcing what we were celebrating. Sister's eyes lit up with amazed joy while she "danced" around on her hands and knees and squealed with delight, and even John had tears in his eyes. Jane had Sister recite some Bible verses she'd memorized, and I gave a little speech about how much she inspired me with her resilience, faith, and exuberant cheer towards life. John presented her with the beautiful certificate we'd created just for her, and we closed with a party with snacks and singing.

It was only many months later when we were saying our tearful goodbyes before moving to South Africa that I began to comprehend the full impact of God's work. Before He intervened, Jane felt only shame for Sister's condition since everyone believed it was caused by a curse. Even though Jane was an intelligent, Christian woman, superstitions run deep, and she somehow bought in to the lie that she was at fault. It broke her heart perpetually to see her beloved daughter shunned. At our going-away party, Jane was one of the designated speakers. My normally composed, soft-spoken friend fought through her tears to shyly express, for the first time ever, how defeated she'd felt before the Lord brought us to give Sister dignity and honor as His precious creation, and one who blessed us all with her contagious joy of life and indomitable spirit. Victory!

~

Maria. Her very name means "bitter. When I first met her, Maria was indeed bitter, and angry, and in excruciating pain. Maria had cervical cancer, another opportunistic disease often affecting women with AIDS. The closest chemotherapy available was in neighboring South Africa, and she could neither financially nor physically afford the journey. In fact, she could not even manage a trip to the clinic about four miles away. She was dependent on another missionary for her one pain pill a day, and saved it until she could no longer bear the agony.

Ncamsile asked if I would visit her and I agreed. We entered her foul-smelling hut, and as my eyes became accustomed to the murky confines of the tiny room, I saw her. Her emaciated frame was curled up under a moth-eaten blanket on a filth-encrusted mattress which was lying on the dirt floor. All I could see was her dark head. There were not even any sheets or pillows to give the utter wretched scene the illusion of decency or dignity. Low moans emanated from her parched lips, and rage from her red-rimmed eyes. Every fiber in my natural being wanted to turn and flee the frightful decay that flooded all my senses. It was those eyes that held me captive. That steely gaze transfixed me, as though she was daring me to walk away, while also warning me not to show any pity whatsoever. I prayed; I stayed.

While Ncamsile made the usual inquiries one makes when there is suffering for which there is no cure, I allowed my eyes to roam while Maria's eyes were not holding my own hostage. I noted the half-filled cup of stale mealie porridge which had attracted both flies and ants; a tin cup almost full of water which too had attracted a visitor—a lone bee floating around the top; and a few mildewing rags. All these were atop a crate, the only other "furniture" in the room. There were a few other miscellaneous containers taking up the remaining space: a plastic basin with a few items of clothing spilling out of it; two or three gallon containers I assumed at one time contained corn meal and maybe sugar and beans; and, incongruously, one clean skirt neatly hung on some sort of peg that protruded from the mud wall.

Once Ncamsile had gathered the bits of information Maria was able share through clenched teeth (yes, she was in pain, no, she was not hungry, yes, her estranged sister and only living relative still refused to visit or help in anyway, yes, I could pray for her), I somehow found the courage to kneel down and gently touch her sweaty forehead and beseech God for His mercy. I was grateful for any small thing in that moment and was immensely relieved that the tension in her body seemed to give way for that brief holy interval.

Thus ended my first, but not my last, visit with Maria. She lived for several more months after that. One time she was even able to crawl outside when my friends Margaret and Sherry were visiting from the US. Margaret's tender prayers seemed to pierce through Maria's defiance while Sherry's gentle ministry of massaging Maria's bony frame with sweet-scented lotion brought us all to tears.

Other visitors were not so lucky, and I was given reports of Maria throwing her cup or bowl at the village women who faithfully tended her as best they could, washing her meager clothing and blanket in the canal, sharing a cup of corn meal mush when they could spare none, and generally showing compassion to the mean-spirited, middle-aged woman in their midst. Even when she felt I had been away too long, she rebuked me harshly. She was not easy to love, but then again, neither was I, and God still bestowed His grace on me.

Time and again we implored Him to heal her, to save her, to give her peace. She claimed to be a Christian but fooled no one. It was simply her cunning attempt to make us help her.

She feared if she confessed the truth, we would visit her no longer. Yet the truth will always come forth, and one day it did.

In spite of their constant proximity to death, or perhaps because of it, as a culture Swazis denied it. Maria was offered the usual platitudes given by those who are afraid to speak the truth. She was promised, in gentle sing-song siSwati, that she would get better and live a long life. Up until then, I had honored their coping mechanism of silence on the matter, afraid myself to open the door to such depths of communal fear and sorrow.

It was only when my friend and missionary nurse, Teresa, suggested I begin to teach them skills in ministering to those approaching death that I was able to summon the fortitude to do so. I began with a rather reluctant Ncamsile and Jane, my closest friends and interpreters. I know it was only because they wanted to please me that they were even willing to try. I coached and I coached and dared to believe we were getting somewhere when they agreed to speak honestly with Maria. The three of us went in for our regular visit…and the two of them froze.

It was time; I heeded the Holy Spirit's urging and asked Maria if she knew where she would go when she died. She said she hoped she would go to Heaven but doubted she would. She knew she was dying, and did not seem at all surprised by my line of questioning, and in fact seemed to welcome it. I took as deep of a breath as I could stand in the fetid air, and allowed the Spirit to begin speaking through me.

I cannot remember all that transpired, but I vividly remember the turning point. Maria was angry with God, and finally admitted it. First, she raged that He did not care about her pain. Next she whined that He did nothing about her sister's refusal to forgive her for the years of hostility between them. It was not easy to listen to her vent but we stood our ground, and finally the root of bitterness was exposed. I asked her if she had any children, and tears formed in her eyes as her bony hand began prodding under the crate for her hidden treasure. It was a ripped black and white photo of her only child, a daughter, as a young adult. This daughter loved Jesus, faithfully attended church, and put her trust in God. This daughter died in her prime. Oh, how Maria hated God after that.

I asked for her daughter's name, and softly and reverently she gave it. I asked if she knew where her daughter was now. Maria replied that she knew with certainty that her God-fearing offspring was in Heaven. I asked if she wanted to see her daughter again. Without hesitation, she replied that she wanted nothing more. I told her the way was through Jesus. She was ready. We prayed. Maria passed a few days after that, but her last few days on earth were peaceful. Her perpetual scowl was replaced with an almost childlike smile. And we rejoiced when we buried her, knowing for certain that she was out of pain, and that as believers we would see her again. *"When the perishable puts on the imperishable, and the mortal puts on immortality, then shall come to pass the saying that is written: 'Death is swallowed up in victory.' ...Thanks be to God, who gives us victory through our Lord Jesus Christ." 1 Corinthians 15:54, 57*

Chapter 11

Eighty-Five Boxes of Macaroni and Cheese

God is the Good Gift Giver.

"...How much more will your Father who is in heaven give good things...?" Matthew 7:11

Our son Jeremy is a sweet, shy introvert. He did make some wonderful friends in Swaziland, but we knew, though he never complained, that he missed American city life, his friends in Arizona, and (to my chagrin) his former diet staple, boxed macaroni and cheese. Two years after we had settled in our new country of residence, we were all excited with the arrival of a team from our home church in Phoenix. The delightful crew was comprised of six teenage girls, three moms, and one of the male church elders.

They came with a gigantic array of wonderful gifts, mostly for the population we served, but also some goodies from home for us. The most memorable of all was one to which John and I were sworn to secrecy until it could be bestowed on our unsuspecting son. Finally, the designated evening arrived, and we were all lounging in chairs, draped over the arms of furniture, or sitting cross-legged on the ground in the spacious and charming living room of our local pastor. At the signal, the six lovely young ladies left the room, while dear Jeremy was still clueless as to what was about to befall him.

Slowly, one by one, the pretty girls, not even trying to stifle their giggles, placed box after box after box of macaroni and cheese at the feet of our blushing, speechless son. This continued for many minutes and the pile grew and grew, as did our hoots of laughter and hearty applause. Jeremy began stammering, "Uh, thank you, thank you," as what else can a young man say while being served in such a glorious manner by six beautiful women? The final tally yielded eighty-five boxes of bounty, lovingly carried all the way from Phoenix, Arizona. Such are the blessings heaped upon those who serve the Lord!

Jeremy was the recipient of another gift in such a hilarious way that it became one of our favorite family stories. We always tried to get away for a few days each year to relax and recoup. One year we took almost a week off to drive to Cape Town, South Africa, and back, sightseeing along the way.

One stop was at a primate sanctuary called "Monkeyland." Monkeys had always been Jeremy's favorite animal, and we were really looking forward to the tour. An informative female guide led the way and introduced the twenty or so people in our group to the various species of mischievous residents, all of which had been in captivity at some point and were not at all afraid of us. It was exhilarating to be so close to the uncaged animals and we were having a great time.

Just before crossing a suspended rope bridge with our tour party, we noticed that Jeremy was no longer with us. With some alarm, we alerted the guide who instructed us to wait where we were while she went in search. My anxiety grew when she didn't return immediately, but finally she came back with a sheepish Jeremy in tow. He was dismayed and embarrassed, and also quite obviously without his glasses, as he explained what had transpired.

He had been observing the antics of some of the primates and hadn't noticed that the rest of us had moved on. In a flash, one of the Vervet monkeys snatched his glasses off of Jeremy's face and ran away with the newly acquired prize. Jeremy had no clue what happened to the spectacles after that. As he exasperatedly explained when he was questioned, "I don't know! I couldn't see!" In fact, since he couldn't see much of anything at that point, he decided to stay put, and that is where the guide found him.

She apologized but also reminded us that the signs at the entrance gave warning that this might happen, and explained that usually the simian culprit would drop the shiny stolen plaything and much later, they would find the shattered evidence. Poor Jeremy didn't much enjoy the rest of our stay, and I kept one hand firmly on my own glasses while practical John tried to figure out what to do. The exhibit employees did try to find the missing glasses, but to no avail. Finally, we had to resume our coastal road trip along the beautiful, aptly-named Garden Route, though Jeremy was quite unable to take in the colorful, majestic scenery.

Once we reached breathtaking Cape Town and located our rather antiquated and quirky hotel, our next order of business was not sightseeing, but to locate the nearest optometrist, who happened to be in a mall not too far away. Jeremy's prescription was an unusual one and we had little hope of getting new lenses for him before we could return to his regular eye doctor back home.

After an interminable wait as it was late on a busy Friday afternoon, a helpful assistant listened to our tale of woe and graciously called the office where Jeremy had gotten his original prescription filled. Our helper agreed that it was highly unlikely they could locate lenses that would match Jeremy's rare needs, but promised she would check with the warehouse and get back to us as soon as she could. We went back to the hotel for the evening, all thoroughly disheartened. But we prayed.

In less than twenty-four hours, our employee friend from the local optometrist's office called with miraculous news. They'd found lenses to match the ones Jeremy had lost! Hastily we piled into the car and made a much more optimistic trip to the mall. In typical Jeremy fashion, he made a quick decision on frames, and we were able to enjoy the rest of our holiday without mishap.

A funny side note: On the same trip, we thoroughly delighted in the antics of the inhabitants of one of the colonies of migrating wild penguins located at the southern tip of

Africa. In fact, it was the highlight of the entire trip for all three of us. After a lifetime of a fanatic affection for monkeys, Jeremy switched allegiance and now claims the penguin as his favorite animal.

~

As I mentioned before, God's blessings rained down on us in our immense garden. One of my favorite yields was the delicious crop of mangoes from at least six trees on our property. We freely shared with those in our little village, but still there were way more than enough to go around. Feeling quite generous, we invited Philemon, who lived just a few miles away, to come and pick some for his family.

He arrived very early the next day, but to our shock, also brought all of his children, and both of his wives, all equipped with long sticks to knock the fruit down, and large containers for the harvest! With all but the two babies, who were tied African-style on their mothers' backs, able to pluck the ripe mangoes, we feared they would wipe the entire crop out, leaving nothing behind for our neighbors or ourselves.

It was one of many dilemmas we faced because of communication mix-ups, and very awkward. We realized our blunder too late. To Swazis, "family" includes a whole slew of extended relatives, which can easily mean hundreds of truly hungry people. Our intent was to bless Philemon's large-enough nuclear family; they heard something else entirely. We did not want to hurt our relationship with them, but we also had to think about the welfare of many others. Thankfully though, they tried to hide their disappointment, and seemed to understand our predicament. While still taking an enormous amount, they didn't quite strip all our trees bare. We were sure God's abundance fed many, many mouths in the days to come!

~

We once received enough donations from a small group of dear little children of friends of ours back in the States, who'd worked hard to earn every cent, for the purchase of two hundred siSwati Bibles. Given that we were ministering in nine different communities, each comprised of hundreds of people, this was quite a windfall. Everyone wanted a Bible, attributing supernatural power to the books even if they were not followers of the Divine Author. Even with this extraordinary abundance, we had to carefully and discretely give only to those we believed would actually read them.

It was strikingly clear that those recipients cherished the gifts. I wish that we of more affluence responded with the reverence and sheer joy that these materially poor Swazis did to God's written Word. One after another, they would caress the books, hold them to their hearts, and lift their hands and voices in praise to the Gift Giver. One sweet sincere woman ran to fetch something from her nearby hut and thrust it into my outstretched hands. It was a torn and rain-stained Bible tract, handed out many years earlier in her son's school classroom, and she'd carefully guarded the treasure ever since. She exclaimed that until now, it was the only piece of God's Word she had, more precious than silver or gold, which she'd read and reread until she had it all memorized. Now she had the entire riches in her hands.

When I was a child, I coveted one of those cheap, pressed-wood airplanes which shot off like an arrow for a few breathless feet when you released the attached rubber band. My single mother and I did not have money for such trinkets, but I did have the simple joy of playing with those my friends received. I had long since lost my sense of awe and wonder in clever toys, but it was rekindled when a friend sent a few of these childhood delights for us to distribute in Africa.

John showed the assembled children the intricacies of good piloting, and they quickly caught on, laughing with glee and running around each other, jubilantly showing off not only their new skills but also one of the few toys they'd ever owned.

Soon, the mothers came out to see what all the commotion was, and proprietarily took the gifts from their children. At first I was outraged at their selfishness. Then I watched as the moms, one by one, tried the new game. As one, their children cheered them on, overjoyed to see their usually staid and exhausted parents giggling and joining in the frivolity. Smiles all around, courtesy of Jesus!

No matter how valiantly we tried, our generosity paled in comparison with that of our Swazi brothers and sisters. We gave from our overflow; they gave what they could not afford.

Even a simple bar of soap was beyond the means of most of our friends, and a heavy, dark green brick of smelly cheap soap called "green bar" was the staple for bathing, laundry, and washing dishes for the majority of households who could afford nothing else. Every little piece of green bar was carefully hoarded and used until there was nothing left of it.

One fine day I had placed my lovingly hand-woven mat on the ground and ignorantly left it there while I went to round up the ladies for our Bible study. Lesson learned—I was dismayed upon my return to find that some rude chicken had unabashedly defecated all over my cherished gift. I was so embarrassed and wanted to just hide the offense, but my ladies were too quick, always on the lookout for my welfare. Their practiced eyes immediately spotted the offending blemish. While I was flustered at my stupidity and worried that they would think I did not care enough for their gift to take decent care of it, I finally realized that they were even more ashamed that one of their chickens had treated me, their honored guest, in such a crude manner.

Over my vehement protests that I would clean it later, several of the ladies picked up leaves and twigs and began determinedly to rid the mat of its blot. One was even more resolute than the others, and did not hesitate. In a flurry of bare feet and long skirts she high-tailed it to her abode and hurriedly returned with a small chunk of her precious green bar and a small cup of equally precious water. With her bare hands and hoarded treasures, she carefully and lovingly restored my mat to its former glory, much to the others' delight, and my humble gratitude.

Mats were one way these precious women with virtually nothing found to bless me. Another was with chickens. For them, giving a chicken was akin to us giving away a month's worth of groceries, knowing there was no replacement coming. It was no small gift, and always presented with much pomp while the others cheered the lavish offering from the sidelines. There was no way I could refuse, even though the scrawny, clucking fowls frankly caused me much private anguish.

Animal lover that I am, being confronted with the harsh realities of the food chain is something I avoid at all costs. Also, I never did learn how to properly hold or transport the creatures, though usually one of the women had pity on me and did the dirty work for me. After my initial journey with an untethered hen in my car, I insisted on some sort of container. Most often, a discarded "Feed My Starving Children" box was proffered (long after its life-giving nourishing contents had been cooked and doled out) and the pathetic creature was placed unceremoniously in the cardboard receptacle, and the top flaps secured before it could escape. Even the box was quite a gift where firewood was a scarce but necessary commodity in a place where no one had electricity, and all meals and warmth came from what they could scavenge to burn.

Off my feathered passenger and I would go, she quietly clucking and bemoaning her fate, and I doing my utmost to focus on my mission of mercy rather than my rider's short lifespan. A mission of mercy it truly was—not for the poor chicken, but for someone in another village, far removed from the gift giver's home. You see, I never could bring myself to actually eat one of the poor creatures so lovingly given to me. Rather, I'd take these occasional extravagant gestures of love to someone who was truly hungry and would appreciate them as food. After all, it is more blessed to give than to receive!

Once a dilemma presented itself that was not so neatly managed, and my poor American guests had to try to explain why they could not take the proffered chicken for their journey home. I'm still not sure the perplexed granny ever truly grasped the complexities of travel by airplane!

Of all the expansive gifts I received, the very best of all was my Swazi name, which I briefly mentioned in Chapter One. I will give this gift the full attention it deserves here. It was a compilation of love bestowed by two of my precious interpreters. Ncamsile insisted I use her last name, Mavuso. In Swazi culture, one's last name, or surname as they term it, holds deep meaning. One's family is a huge part of one's identity, designating where one was born, who one's clan is, and any number of other characteristics relating to that clan, including clan alliances and history. So by giving me her surname, Ncamsile was honoring me in the most powerful way she knew how.

It was Fikile who gave me my first name, or forename as it is called in Swaziland. We were in the kitchen, she stirring something in the pot and I doing what I do best in the kitchen—staying out of the way and encouraging the real cooks—when Fikile decided it was time for me to have a Swazi name. After a brief conference in siSwati with another Swazi friend who was tending to the oven contents, they smilingly agreed that I should be called "Siphiwe," which means "gift."

Every good gift and every perfect gift is from above...James 1:17. "Ngiyabonga, Babe." "Thank you, Daddy."

Chapter 12

"All I know is that I love Jesus and that Jesus loves me."

God is Hope.

"This I recall to my mind, therefore I have hope. Through the Lord's mercies we are not consumed, because His compassions fail not." Lamentations 3:21-22

The ancient ones, those rare survivors who have seen so much; lived through two kings; withstood the Swazi version of the plague of locusts; and endured the loss of children and grandchildren to the scourge of AIDS, disease and poverty, had so many stories to tell of it all. Oh, how I loved them, those "bogogo" (grannies) in their multiple layers of colorful skirts and blanket shawls for warmth and comfort when there was no one left to hug or hold them.

Mayiwase was eighty-five years old, though she could not remember her birth date or birth year. Instead, she relied on our report after we read her Swazi I.D., rescued from somewhere in the billows of her skirts. Her gait was slow, aided with a walking stick, but her back was ramrod straight, and she could still balance quite a load on her head in spite of her thin, frail frame. Despite her age, she never missed a Bible study on Tuesdays, or church on Sundays. They were her only social interactions as she lived alone and was rarely visited by anyone. It was more than loneliness that drove her to her faithful attendance though; she loved the Lord.

She patiently waited each week until all the other ladies shared their answers to the icebreaker question. Oh, how the women in that group loved to talk! A simple question elicited a longwinded, rambling account that might or might not have answered the original question, but did serve to allow each member to share whatever was on her heart since she had a captive audience. More often than not, the narrative often featured the teller in some virtuous role.

For a while I ignored the imperious eye rolls and bored expressions the others rudely displayed when it was finally Mayiwase's turn. We all knew exactly what she would say. Regardless of the question, which her old ears could never quite make out anyway, her proclamation was always exactly the same. One day, I'd had enough of the superior attitudes of the others, and demanded that they afford her the respect due to her as an elderly woman and as a sister in Christ. I went further to praise this steadfast grandmother, who was an example to us all of how to give a succinct and God-honoring testimony. What unfailingly came from her sweet lips was, "I can't see and I can't hear. All I know is that I love Jesus and Jesus loves me." Amen!

From the revealing sunrise peeping through the mango and papaya trees to the merciful red sunset behind the moringa plantation, we were face to face with suffering. There was no escaping it, no turning away, no pretending for even one brief interval of respite that there was not a mass of humanity at our doorstep, and for miles and miles and miles beyond, who lived lives of utter desperation and despair.

Misery-filled eyes from our hungry/sick/abused/marginalized neighbors greeted us each new dawn and followed us everywhere we went. Even though we lived quite frugally by middle-class American standards, to them we were an endless source of wealth. Children begged for money as they rubbed their swollen tummies in a circular motion and repeated the mantra in which they had been coached from toddlerhood, "I am hungry." Adults were more practiced and humbly presented their problems, tacitly asking if we could help while never being rude enough to come out and ask.

We wrestled, oh, how we wrestled with it all. Were we doing enough? Were we doing too much? Were we doing the right things? Were we doing more harm than good?

It was too much to humanly bear. The demands far surpassed our human abilities, and it was so tempting to focus on the gaping needs in front of us rather than the All-Sufficient God. Even our loved ones back home didn't really want to hear the physical realities for very long. My long, anguished emails were often met with short platitudes or worse, ignored. In fact, you may wish I would move on to a happier story right now; so maybe you understand a bit about our dilemma.

When we were asked in front of our home church crowd in Phoenix before moving to Africa what our biggest wish was, I passionately and sincerely did not hesitate to respond, "To glorify God." The tension was this: How was I to glorify a sovereign Lord while at the same time communicating with our supporters just how truly awful things were? It became so difficult to be immersed in such wretchedness and still report on a good and loving God. My faith never faltered, but my emotions did. I was face to face with hell, crying out to catch glimpses of Heaven.

> *As a deer pants for the water brooks, so pants my soul for you, O God... My tears have been my food day and night, while they continually say to me, "Where is your God?" ...Why are you cast down, O my soul, and why are you disquieted within me? Hope in God; for I shall yet praise Him, my salvation.* Psalm 42:1, 3, 5

"Look at Me; look at Me," my Savior, my Hope would call to me. And I would sing praise songs to Him, and He would restore my soul with songs of hope, and walk with me through the valley yet another day.

I came to dread the frequent "knock, knocks" on our battered kitchen screen door. Inevitably it was someone needing something, and more often than not we simply could not provide.

With windows wide open to allow fresh air into the stifling heat of our concrete home, there was no hiding and no avoiding the parade of visitors. Even if we were away, they would patiently sit under a shade tree and wait until our car rounded the bend.

The most common request was for money for education. Education was a highly-prized commodity in a country where it was neither free nor even affordable for so many. Children in classrooms knew that they were the lucky ones, and sat up straight in their chairs, giving respectful obeisance to their strict teachers. Even the most dilapidated of schools had some sort of playground, and while the favored ones frolicked happily inside the grounds, other less fortunate youngsters peered longingly through the holes in the fences. Everyone knew education was the key to a better life.

Sometimes it was an adult, pleading through Phinda, who doubled as our interpreter on such occasions, for their young child. Other times it would be an older teenager, dressed in his or her best clothes, carrying a neatly-typed or handwritten letter of introduction. Each time we welcomed them, regretfully explained that we truthfully couldn't even afford to put our own children through school, and then we did what we were there to do. We pointed to the Lord. We taught them to pray. We could not meet their needs, but we knew Someone who could. We asked if they knew Jesus, and if they had a saving relationship with Him. If they did, we'd join hands and cry out to Him for provision. If they did not, we'd exhort them to repent and ask Him into their hearts, lives, and present circumstances of need. Glorious were those days that, while they did not receive what they'd come for, they walked away with so much more—the hope of eternal life. *"Silver and gold I do not have, but what I do have I give to you..."* Acts 3:6

―

Heads bowed, arms outstretched to heaven, my Swazi sisters and brothers cried out to God with a fundamental urgency, not for a nicer car or a better job, but simply for their daily bread, or to wake up breathing the next day. They knew with a certainty that He was their only source, their only hope.

―

Children are children worldwide. I used to love to attend the preschool graduations in our area. One by one the adorable curly-haired tots were called forward to state their names, ages, and what they wanted to be when they grew up. In sing-song voices, still unaccustomed to the English language in which they were expected to respond, but clearly having practiced their answers multiple times, they would shout, "Police!" "Teacher!" "Soldier!" "Nurse!" and occasionally, "Pastor!" as the few parents and relatives who attended clapped and cheered loudly as though to somehow compensate for the majority who either could not be there, or who didn't care enough to be. The children valiantly carried on and dreamed their dreams.

As part of the many interviews I conducted with the rural women I came to admire and love so deeply, I would often ask the ladies what their childhood dreams had been, and what their dreams were now. The latter was a revolutionary question to ask my downtrodden, worn out, demoralized sisters. They had probably not been asked that question since their preschool days, if they were lucky enough to attend, or perhaps never before in their lives if not. Older girls and women were not taught to dream, but simply to obey and to perform their traditional back-breaking chores of servitude day in and day out, year after year.

Invariably the responses were the same -- first, incomprehension of what was being asked. Ncamsile would patiently explain each time, having been by my side through numerous such interviews, and understanding not only the question, but also my intent to affirm them as feeling human beings, to encourage, to care. Once understanding dawned on their disbelieving faces and in their weary hearts, the question was repeated by my faithful friend, and we could almost see the years of practiced dulling of emotions fall away, and tears would form in the corner of grateful dark brown eyes.

When we first started this line of questioning, I had anticipated dreams of economic prosperity, or faithful husbands who didn't beat them, or health. And yes, those were certainly requests for prayers. I optimistically hoped that some might dream of literacy, or evangelism, or starting a business. But the previously unspoken dreams of these darling women were unfailingly the same. I had learned to sit silently while they probed their deepest, long-suppressed hearts' desires. They were realists. Maybe they didn't know the statistics about the low life expectancy in that part of the globe, but they were astute observers of their narrow world, and knew that their chances of raising their children to adulthood were far from certain. After reflecting, every single one softly replied that she hoped her children would follow the Lord…after she died.

Children grew up quickly there. It was common to see a five-year-old child caring for an infant or toddler sibling in the absence of a parent. Child heads of households were routinely ten-year-olds. Prepubescent girls were given in marriage. Their dreams faded quickly in the heavy demands of adult responsibilities, but not their indomitable hope that God might come to their aid.

I once prayed with a darling five-year-old girl. Her story was not unfamiliar; I'd heard variations of it too many times. Her mother had recently died, and her alcoholic, unemployed father had quickly taken another woman. The new "wife" did not want the other woman's child around, so the man simply dropped his daughter off at her grandmother's without a backward glance. This child's precious shy plea was that her daddy would quit drinking and would love her again. As I reassured her that Jesus would always love her, I was compelled to silently beg that she would truly come to know the endless love of her heavenly Father.

Foolish pride in my own ability versus humble trust in His. Human suffering juxtaposed with an All-Powerful Creator. Age-old conundrums. My Daddy listened patiently to my questioning, held me when I railed against the injustice, and taught me, through those I was supposed to be teaching, the art of enduring faith—the *"substance of things hoped for, the evidence of things not seen"* (Hebrews 11:1). He reassured me of our place in eternity, where *"God will wipe away every tear from [our] eyes; there shall be no more death, nor sorrow, nor crying. There shall be no more pain, for the former things [will] pass away"* (Revelation 21:4)."

Philemon, ever my unlikely and unknowing tutor, gave me new insight into the psyche of those whose lives are all about survival. The countryside in Swaziland is breathtakingly beautiful, yet none of my Swazi friends seemed to appreciate what to me was God's amazing gift of His creation, there for our pleasure. In fact, I decided that in my "superior" knowledge, I needed to teach them to be thankful for the magnificent natural surroundings into which they'd been born.

One day, I was driving my usual carload full, including Philemon, to evening intercessory prayer at the church. My passengers began chuckling as one to see a "burn" on the horizon. My reputation was well known for an almost addiction to watching those walls of fire that were the sugar cane fields being prepared for harvest. They could never comprehend my awe at what was such a common sight to them, since they'd witnessed those towering, massive infernos nine months of the year since birth, but they found endless amusement in my obsession and compulsion to pull off to the side of the road and stare transfixed for fifteen or so minutes until the violent crackling flames died down to dull embers. In fact, as I was also compulsive about being on time in a country where no one else cared, it was common knowledge that if I was late anywhere, it was because I'd come upon a mesmerizing fire!

Few dared to counter me, especially in my own vehicle, but when I jokingly suggested we stop to admire the view, Philemon very seriously replied, "We must not get too attached to the things of this fallen world, but rather we must focus on things of eternity." I drove straight to the prayer meeting.

My journal entry one day stated, "This is too hard. I am ready to quit." The next morning, I received an email notification that a long-time friend had passed after a long battle with cancer. He had been a joyful Christian, a doting husband and father, and an uncomplaining servant. Through our grief, we all also had the blessed peace of knowing that Wayne was now rejoicing to see Jesus face to face in heaven. God's message to me that day was piercingly clear. "Quit complaining and get back to work. Others need the hope I have given you. There are souls to be saved and I've chosen you to show them the way." Ironically, through the loss of a wonderful brother, He lifted my spirits and filled me with His joyful purpose once again.

It was often like that. Just when I felt like I could carry on no further, I'd receive a cheerful email from a long-lost friend, or a rare greeting card in the mail with timely words of encouragement. There was the day I spotted, through my tears, a graceful crane in a field, causing me to wonder in His gracious beauty. On another occasion I came upon a family of newborn warthogs, my favorite African animal because they make me laugh with their comical, grinning faces. In so many creative ways, He reminded me that He was there, that His burden is light, and that His love is extravagant. Always, my faithful husband was there to hold me when I cried. And always, my Daddy sweetly whispered, "Press on, beloved daughter, press on."

We had buried Nonhlanhla's baby daughter a few months earlier, and now Nonhlanhla herself seemed to be failing. Normally robust, she had become listless, refused food, and was wasting away. Each time I visited her community, I noted helplessly that she was slipping further and further away from us.

I will never forget one day when we spotted her sitting in the mud, in the pouring rain, about a hundred yards from the village. Somehow she had summoned the strength and desire to live, long enough to hitch a ride to the community clinic. On her return, the "khombi," as the inexpensive public transportation vans were called, had unceremoniously dropped her off on the paved road, leaving her alone to make her way painfully down the dirt road leading to her home. When she could go no more than a few yards on her wobbly legs, she simply sat down, resigned to her fate. As soon as we saw her plight, Ncamsile, my visiting friend Elizabeth, and I jumped into my car to go rescue her, and between the three of us we got her drenched form into the vehicle and delivered her to some relatives who could care for her properly.

I saw Nonhlanhla for what I was sure was the last time when she came to the Christmas party I was hosting for the ladies at the church. I couldn't believe she was even there, and when the activity time came, and each lady was instructed to choose a partner and to take turns massaging each other's well-worn servant hands, I rushed to her side. She was sitting on the floor, leaning against a wall, and I gently took her skeleton hands in my mine and tried unsuccessfully to hold back my tears as I ministered to her in this small way. Her wan smile told me that she understood my love.

I thought of Nonhlanhla often that year when we were back in the US celebrating the birth of the Savior, and thanked Him that at least I was assured of her salvation. The opulent material wealth that is America was that year a garish reminder of the tragedy of my friend's hard life back in Swaziland, without even decent medical care, and I was all too ready to return to the simpler life and harsh realities to which I was now more accustomed. At least, life seemed real and vital in southern Africa, and not wasted so much on frivolous vanities and superficial indulgences. Yes, I was angry.

I was so afraid to return to Nonhlanhla's village—afraid of my own emotions, afraid to hear how she'd died, afraid to hear who else might have passed in my absence. "Oh, ye of little faith." There she was, coming out to greet me! Nonhlanhla was healed! Thanks to a shipment of the necessary medication, she was undergoing the regimen to battle tuberculosis, and thanks to Jehovah Rapha, she was getting stronger every day!

Just as my sister had been stuck in the miry mud a few months earlier, I'd been stuck in the miry mud of despair. Just as we'd lifted her out, He'd lifted me out, and hope soared in my heart that day!

Months later, an absolutely chubby and hearty Nonhlanhla led the way during our monthly hospital visit. She testified boldly of how Jesus had healed her, and many patients were encouraged that day to believe they could be healthy and whole again. So I testify today. May you likewise be encouraged and filled with hope.

Chapter 13

Boo Boos and Brushing the Dirt Off

God is the Refiner.

> "He will sit as a refiner and purifier of silver; He will purify the sons of Levi, and purge them as gold and silver, that they may offer to the LORD an offering in righteousness."
> Malachi 3:3

Many years have passed since my own children were small, but a mother never really forgets those exhausting, challenging, precious and fleeting years. Like most moms, I did my very best, yet made many mistakes along the way and fervently prayed that my sons' heavenly Father would fill in the gaps where we failed as earthly parents. I was one of those moms who thoroughly researched and agonized over every parenting technique, and carefully chose between the myriad of options available for everything between breast or bottle feeding, immunizations or not, cloth or disposable diapers, homemade baby food versus store-bought jars, and Christian preschool versus one with a more educational slant. We were so blessed to have such a wealth of knowledge and resources available to us.

It has been with great interest that I observed mothers in a culture vastly different than my own. Most could not read, and certainly did not have access to the Internet. Immunizations were coveted in a land facing so many deadly diseases. Breastfeeding was the only way they knew as bottles and formula would have been an exorbitant expense when it was all a mommy could do to keep her own body replenished with enough calories to feed her baby as well. I watched with admiration time and time again as a woman gracefully and casually slung a baby on her back, then swiftly and efficiently secured a blanket around the tot and tied the corners under her own breasts, freeing her hands for the many chores ahead of her for the day.

There were other differences as well. Babies learned early on not to cry. Swazi mothers were very skilled at hushing their wee ones, the baby's earliest training in stoic Swazi resignation to the many hard things over which they felt no control. I learned as I watched.

One afternoon, a small group of us were sitting or reclining on our grass mats or blankets under a shade tree, discussing our families, as women are prone to do. Ncamsile's sleepy-eyed toddler had just woken from his nap on his mama's lap, and spied some playmates nearby. Still drowsy, he was nevertheless eager to reach the other kids, and in his haste, tripped over the giant root of a tree and took a pretty hard fall. It took every ounce of self-control I had not to rush over to pick him up and soothe him when the other women seemed to deliberately ignore his distressed wails. I was frustrated, concerned, and angry with the seeming lack of basic maternal compassion from the ladies who casually continued to chatter away. He had fallen hard enough that I even feared he had broken a bone, and I definitely saw blood. I was even more appalled when Ncamsile, who I considered a very loving mother, began laughing in his direction.

Slowly, comprehension dawned. This young boy, and all his comrades, would face pain much worse than bloody knees and elbows. They would lose loved ones frequently and attend many funerals at an early age; violence would more than likely be a part of their lives; storms would destroy their shelter, and drought would ravage their family gardens so that there would be many days when they went to bed hungry; crocodiles and highly venomous snakes could take away their playmates' lives in an instant. These resolute mothers knew that all too soon, they themselves might not be around to brush the dirt off and kiss the boo-boos, so they were lovingly preparing their offspring in the best way they knew how to withstand the onslaughts of life by pretending to ignore relatively minor pain.

As I grappled with the complexities of the unfairness of life, how to mesh the best of two cultures in parenting, and how to get Thabiso medical help if his wounds became infected, the mothers continued gabbing, Thabiso ceased crying, and Ncamsile gently but firmly pushed him back into the fray.

My heavenly Father will ALWAYS be there to comfort me when I need Him. Yet He also allows the hard things of life in this fallen world to strengthen me for His calling, and to mold me into His image. Because He loves me.

～

Countless times in Swaziland God chiseled away at my self-perceived "rights." I was tested time after painful time about what I truly needed rather than what I was taught in my affluent country that everyone deserved. As my husband, in his forthright, no-nonsense way, truthfully retorts, "We deserve death." *For the wages of sin is death…*Romans 6:23, and *"…all have sinned, and fall short of the glory of God."* Romans 3:23. Each time my brokenness came, He filled me with His inexpressible joy. It was the humbled vessel knowing, absolutely knowing, that nothing was needed other than Him, and that He was more than enough.

～

I will never forget the reverse culture shock of our first trip back to the USA. After one and one half years away, we felt God calling us to go back for a visit with our elderly and ailing parents, supporters wanting to hear face-to-face how we were using their hard-earned donations, and a passion on our part to share not only the vital needs but also the wonderful ways in which God was at work in Swaziland.

Our first day back was the most startling. As I quipped only half-jokingly to our home church crowd, all the white faces in the congregation were a bit scary. We struggled to keep up with the fast pace—on the freeways, in the hustle and bustle of public places, and even in casual conversations, which to our Africa-fresh ears seemed abrupt and terse to the point of rudeness.

John, Jeremy, and I all stood in a formerly familiar fast food restaurant staring bewilderedly at the vast array of choices on the menu while impatient patrons rushed past us to the counter. Later, a friend found me in a different check-out line, still thoroughly jet-lagged and completely unable to figure out how to use my credit card in machines that were newer models than when we'd left. Not only I, but also those in line behind me, breathed a sigh of relief when Jenni mercifully took the card from my trembling hand and with a practiced touch, swiped it through the contraption.

I somehow managed to keep my composure through the strident voices, the harsh synthetic lights, and the cacophony of noise...until I dazedly wandered the aisles of a retail giant's aisles and was confronted with three long, overstocked, excessive rows of extravagant inessentials...for dogs and cats. I lost it then and there, amidst the squeaky toys and doggy sweaters, sobbing over the contrast between hungry children and pampered, coddled pets.

I cried not only for the hungry bellies I had left behind, but also for the spiritual poverty juxtaposed with the material wealth in my home country. The "first world problems" of the wrong coffee confection being served, of a restaurant that still did not serve gluten-free food, or of the challenges of finding a decent place for a pedicure pierced me with grief, for my Swazi brethren as well as for my blindly frivolous American brothers and sisters. Most of all I, grieved because secretly, a guilty part of me missed the life of ordering whatever I wanted in a restaurant, sitting in a plush movie theater seeing the latest flick with my family, being blissfully unaware of the taken-for-granted comfort of central air-conditioning and heating, or yes, buying something frivolous for my dogs. I especially missed singing praise songs in English in church with old friends. Yet even as I enjoyed the ease of old familiarity, I simultaneously longed to be back to our simpler lives with our more peaceable and peaceful Swazi companions. I knew then that what a missionary friend had warned us was true. We were forever "freaks." We would never again fit in completely in either world, our hearts were torn asunder, and we were qualified exclusively to yearn for our only true home: Heaven.

While God was busy scouring my soul, He was also heightening my passion to disciple the Swazi women, as my eyes were wide open now to the transformational power of His Kingdom culture. Through immersion in a foreign culture, I could see more clearly both the godly and the perverse in my own culture as well as in theirs. Clearly His ways, His wisdom, and His order were the ONLY answer to the fallen human condition and depraved earthly cultures, but with spiritual rebirth and renewal came abundant life. I became more zealous than ever for revolution in my own heart and in the hearts and lives of those whom God had placed in our care. I knew God's purifying, enlightening Word was the source of all that we all so desperately needed, and so I pursued discipleship with increasing fervor, coupled with and fueled by depths of love for the Refiner I could never have even dreamed of before.

Discipleship takes time. Jesus has been infinitely tender and patient with me, walking beside me every step of the way through the Refiner's fire. He's not finished with me yet. My heart's desire was to model His gentle perseverance with my own precious chocolate-eyed disciples with their long, swaying skirts, scarf-encased heads, and strong backs and hearts. He had graced me with these women, and allowed me to be sharpened by them as well. We had much to teach each other, my Swazi sisters and I. As Ncamsile and I were discussing these matters one day, she taught me an apropos Swazi proverb. It goes something like this: "When a dog dies, the fleas don't leave it all at once." In other words, once we die to our earthly selves and become new in Christ Jesus, it takes a little while before all the junk falls off!

So many days, I marveled at the exotic life God allowed us to live, while other days I chuckled to myself at how mundane life could be on the mission field. While we rarely reported such in our newsletters, much of our time was spent shopping for food and cooking it, filling the tank with gasoline, washing the dishes, paying the bills, handling ministry correspondence and administrative tasks, and other boring, tedious, and common work that is just a part of life.

Yet it was in these very menial tasks that so much of God's training took place. Dishes had to be washed by hand as dishwashers had not yet made it to rural Swaziland, giving me plenty of time to reflect on the holiness of simple, everyday tasks done unto the Lord. We drove many, many kilometers to reach far-flung rural villages, allowing many heart-to-heart talks with the Lord or glorious times of singing praise songs to Him on the road. Responding to ministry emails necessitated pondering what God had done and was doing in us and through us. The bills could not be paid online or even through the mail, meaning John had to drive into town regularly to take care of business. In the process, he developed many relationships there with his friendly and joking ways. He was very adept at slipping Jesus into everyday conversations and challenging the status quo.

In all these things He was shaping us and using us to shape the lives, worldview, and hearts of others.

God continues His mighty work in all of our lives, but our season in Swaziland was finite. Deep down, I knew our work there was finished, and that it was time for my sisters to put into practice all that I'd taught them in the past three and one half years. Through our many goodbye tears and anguished sobbing sessions where we literally drenched each other's clothing, I surrendered once again. I relinquished my beloved Swazi sisters into His capable hands, and my own grieving heart unto His will. The call to move on came many months before we were to leave, and He revealed His plans to us step-by-painful-step, exhorting me to trust Him even when the way was not yet clear to my weeping eyes.

The old adage is true: He never closes one door without opening another. He was taking us on a new adventure, a new path of refinement, and a new country of residence. South Africa waited, with new trials and new victories, and I was so thankful that we would still be close enough to visit our beloved Swaziland, just across the border, several times a year.

This was small consolation to the women in all my Bible study groups. They were all too intimate with painful goodbyes, but not so much with joyous reunions. Despite my sincere reassurances that I would be back to visit many times, I knew they truly did not believe we would ever see one another again this side of heaven. I became concerned that they had become too emotionally dependent on me rather than on God, and decided I needed to openly address their possibly misplaced allegiance. Oh, how my heart soared when Elizabeth, our resident "Jeremiah" in one of our groups, gave one of her no-nonsense deliveries. She forcefully reminded the ladies,

"Pastor Kay has taught us what we need and now it is up to us to apply it!" Yes!

⁓

The children had long ago given me their own moniker, in honest, childlike fashion, calling things as they saw them. My full "title" became Gogo Umfundisi Umlungu Sweetie, or "Grandmother Pastor White-Person Candy." Even in my early fifties, I was one of the oldest people they knew, thus the "granny" banner. I chose to receive it in the manner in which it was applied, with the respect due to older persons, though inwardly I alternately cringed and chuckled to myself!

"Umfundisi" was what everyone, old and young alike, insisted on calling me. The closest English translation is "pastor," but the Swazi meaning is also infused with the meaning of teacher. I came to accept that that truly was my role with them, that they were honoring me, and that I would be rude to protest, even though I was grossly uncomfortable with anyone being honored other than my Lord Jesus.

"Umlungu" (white person) was even more uncomfortable to me, as I tried so hard to portray our similarities rather than those things that set us apart. Yet I knew that for them, I truly looked very, very different from everyone else, and it was simply their way of distinguishing me from the rest.

"Sweetie" is an Anglicized term used by African children accustomed to American missionaries bringing them candy. Many a short-term team passed out "sweeties," and the children came to associate good things to eat and fun times with white people in general. Whether that is a good or bad thing is a topic for another day.

For many years, in the land of burning sugar cane and warm smiles, I was greeted by the lilting voices of children chanting, "Gogo Umfundisi Umlungu Sweetie" or shortened variations of such, long before I arrived in the villages. Their sweet serenade heralded my arrival and welcomed me through my open car windows, and I was blessed. This loving refrain was one of the last things I heard as we said our farewells.

Chapter 14

Joy on a Grass Mat

God is Joy.

He will yet fill your mouth with laughing, and your lips with rejoicing." Job 8:21

Joy. Our great God is Joy, and He gives immense joy even in the midst of enormous suffering. My Swazi sisters exude joy, inexplicable except for the life of Christ Jesus in them. And I was blessed beyond measure to abide in His joy, through knowing and growing with them.

The happiest times I ever had were sitting among them on a grass mat, under a huge shade tree, while kids and chickens and flies buzzed around us. We discussed the weather, our children, births and deaths, and most of all, our Lord Jesus Christ. We laughed together, and oh, how they could laugh wholeheartedly. We wept together, crying out to Jesus, and oh, how they could weep wholeheartedly. And we sang together, those beautiful Swazi praise and worship songs, their glorious voices drowning out my own, which will only be glorious in heaven!

Relationships take time. God granted me the blessing of sufficient time to gain the trust of my Swazi sisters, and then to begin speaking into their lives through His golden Word, and finally to share in their sorrows and in their joys.

The very first time I started ministering in one of the villages, neither the ladies nor I knew what to expect. I had prayerfully prepared the first of many lessons I would teach them from stories of women in the Bible. Each lesson would consist of first reading the Bible story together, then my expounding on it, and finally discussing life-application questions.

My interpreter and I arrived, both excited, and both nervous. We asked one of the village children to locate our contact person, Rose, who then sent other children to call the ladies to the meeting. I was eager to start and a bit taken aback at having to wait, when we had clearly given the time we should start. Of course, I realized later that they did not live by the clock, and simply knew it was time to gather when they saw me coming, or when they were summoned.

We were told that the ladies were getting ready, which I also later learned meant washing up and changing clothes, before coming to "church." It was a sign of respect for both the

Lord and for me, as water was scarce, had to be carried from the canal, and in winter months was quite cold. It took years for me to convince them that the Lord and I both loved them just as they were.

While the others were putting on their finest, our hostess dispatched an older child to find the only "chairs" in the community. One was an upturned bucket with holes in it, and the other was a wooden crate covered in spider webs and dirt, which were hastily wiped clean. Every action indicated a high level of undeserved esteem given to me, the white teacher who "stooped so low" as to come into their village. My heart cried out to help them understand that I was no better than they, and that it was I who was honored to be in their presence, and that Jesus Christ Himself wished to lift them up.

After thirty minutes or so, they began arriving singly and in shy groups, not daring to make eye contact, and silently spreading out their grass mats on the ground well away from where we gingerly perched on our seats of honor. In spite of their reticence, I could sense their high spirits, and that gave me the encouragement I needed to set aside my own qualms, and to begin our journey of life together.

Several weeks later, an old granny in the village gifted me with my very first grass mat, and each visit thereafter I determined to further bridge the physical, social, and cultural gap between us. Each visit I painstakingly decreased the space between us on the ground inch by inch, and they became increasingly more comfortable as the distance between us went from many yards to a mere few feet.

The real breakthrough came, however, many months later when one elderly woman arrived late, and there was simply no room for her on any of the grass mats the women shared. I was in the middle of teaching, and thought nothing of motioning for her to come and sit beside me on my own spacious and lonely mat. I quickly realized the profound implications of such a move when I saw the startled hesitancy, not only on her weathered face but also on the faces of the two dozen or so other precious faces before me.

Time seemed to stand still with everyone frozen into place until Ncamsile, as yet unknown to me but already exhibiting her God-given leadership and inspired wisdom far beyond the narrow confines of her life circumstances, broke the silence by encouraging the grandmother to acquiesce. The invisible wall between blacks and whites, between haves and have-nots, between teacher and disciples, irrevocably came tumbling down that day, and I inwardly rejoiced!

God lavished His joy on us in other ways as well. I can think of no perks in corporate America that come close to the delight of spotting giraffes, zebra, elephants, and monkeys on the way to work. Nor could the wonderful assortment of restaurants, movie theaters, and other forms of entertainment John and I took advantage of for our date nights in the United States begin to compare with our date nights hiding out from inquisitive eyes and the incessant demands between fields of sugar cane, munching popcorn together under the brilliant stars of the southern hemisphere, admiring the dancing fireflies, and listening to the croaking of the African toads nearby.

None of the accolades or awards bestowed on me in my former career could approach the honor of being asked to name the babies of some of my Swazi sisters. One of those babies was the last born of Ncamsile, sister of my heart. She went into labor while leading the Moms in Prayer group in her village. After faithfully carrying out her duties through to the very last "Amen," she entered her mud hut, accompanied by two neighbors, and gave birth. There was no doubt in my mind that this baby boy was to be christened "Mkhuleko." "Prayer Warrior!"

And I have seen no place on earth as naturally vibrant and beautiful with lush foliage, rampant tropical flowers, brightly-colored birds, rolling green hills, and dark red soil. I only had to open my eyes for my heart to be flooded with joy in God's glorious creation each and every day.

To this day, neither John nor I can speak of the following without tears springing to our eyes. These are tears of such deep, complex emotions that I myself am unable to explain them fully, though perhaps as I describe the event as it unfolded, you will get a glimpse of the riches of sorrow and of joy bestowed on us that day.

The poorest of the poor villages in which we served, the one all the others looked down upon with abject pity at best, and with derisive scorn at worst, asked to give us a farewell party. These precious women literally starved themselves to shower us with gifts of love. Just as I had no idea what to expect three and a half years earlier when I first came to teach them God's Word, I again could not fathom what was in store for us.

Ever the punctual American, I arrived at the designated time, though John wisely came later. Our hostesses were nowhere in sight, so I resigned myself to wait on a large rock as I was told by a friendly male villager that they had gone to town and would be back "soon." Already I felt pangs of guilt, suspecting that the trip to town was for our benefit, and knowing that even the fee for public transportation there and back cost them dearly. My distress rose further as I spied them all carrying heavy burdens on their heads, gleefully singing and laughing as they approached on the now achingly familiar and dear dirt road into the community.

Love was the force that enabled me to choke back my tears and to join in the gaiety. Amid giggling whispers, they began unwrapping their purchases, first begging me not to look, and then abashedly asking me to help wrap them, as none of them had a clue how to do it, never having opportunity or reason to, but somehow knowing it was done. How could I help but smile as I chuckled at their admonition to wrap but not peek— a request obviously ridiculous to us all!

It became even more comical as I realized they owned neither tape nor scissors, but finally one brought me a dull knife and I made do using the price stickers from the gifts as tape, realizing that the sheer cost of the wrapping paper alone was an exorbitant expenditure for women who used scraps of newspaper or leaves for toilet paper and who scribbled notes with twigs in the dirt. Writing paper was a treasure allocated only to those children able to attend school through charitable donations.

Somehow through the contagious hilarity, we jointly accomplished the task of wrapping, and I was gaily escorted to the designated party site at the edge of the village. More villagers began arriving, and soon the place was overflowing for the festivities.

Once John arrived, the celebration began in earnest. We were flabbergasted at how well organized they were, with so many thoughtful details in place. There was an official master of ceremonies, the daughter of the local headwoman. She formally introduced one dear woman after another, as each nervously but determinedly spoke in front of the crowd about what we'd meant in their lives. The children had been taught a new song dedicated to us, complete with our names in the lyrics. After the high-pitched voices subsided, it was time for food, and no one went hungry that day. John and I even received our favorite soft drinks, while they only drank the same dirty water they always did, albeit in special "chalices" carefully horded for the occasion. For months I'd conscientiously washed and saved all my yogurt containers, passing them on to Ncamsile who'd requested them, thinking she was only using them as cups for her own little family. This day they appeared as the finest china, all matching vessels for the occasion!

I sobbed as we unwrapped the presents, and did my best to act surprised in front of the multitude, as only a few of us were privy to the fact that I'd just wrapped them through laughter a couple of hours earlier. I cried seeing the nice dishes, brand new pots and pans, and an assortment of all the other things they dreamed of having but would never own for their own homes. I cried knowing they were lovingly releasing us through these costly items to move to our new home, far, far away from them. I cried because I was so undeserving of their sacrificial giving and love, love they poured out mirroring the undeserved and sacrificial gift of love from Jesus. They were tears of sorrow… and of inexpressible joy.

As I mentioned before, I pray you will find me singing praise songs to the Lord of lords with my Swazi sisters, who have the most beautiful voices in the world, and I will dance with them, and I will invite you to join us. I've been through the fire, and I thank God that He loves me enough to continue to shape me in His image, and that He will never let me go until I see Him face to face. This is Gogo Umfundisi Umlungu Sweetie Siphiwe Mavuso, signing out.

Postlude: Ncamsile's Story

Author's note: Shadrach, Meshach, and Abednego did not go through the fire alone but rather had each other. Likewise, I did not go through the fire alone. God gave me precious companions. The amazing women who worked as my interpreters became so much more to me; they became dear friends and partners in ministry. Ncamsile became my closest friend, and the sister of my heart. In some ways, her life is representative of rural Swazi women, and yet in three important ways she is unusual. By God's grace she escaped the ravages of disease, sexual abuse, and illiteracy that plague so many. In addition to assisting me in interviewing over 60 Swazi women for their histories (tales for another day!) she shared her own account with me. The following is a compilation of her oral interview and recorded testimony. Here is her story.

Hello, Saints. I greet you in the Name of Jesus. I would like to express myself towards what God has done to me. I am Ncamsile Dudu Mavuso. I was born on April 4, 1976.

I am the mother of six children, two girls and four boys. My firstborn, second-born, third-born, and fourth-born children all have different fathers. My fifth and sixth-born are from another man. Men promised to care for me and my children but I do not know where any of them are. So I am a single mother.

My father kept two wives and five other women by whom he had children. My mother was one of the five other women. My father produced eleven children and nine are still living. My mother gave birth to four children and two are still living.

My mother lived a vagabond life and I never saw her until after I gave birth to my own first two children.

My granny raised me and paid for my school fees so I could complete high school. She was good to me. My father and mother are both dead. My stepmother is the only one surviving of all my father's women. My granny also passed.

My stepmother chased me away from our family homestead because I was having too many children. She did give me a little land close by but I could not afford to build. For a long time, my oldest children stayed with her so they could attend school. I live across the country where I can find enough work to scrape by to support them. It is very hard being apart from them but it is all we can do. I work whenever I can. Sometimes I am hired as a day laborer to weed in the sugar cane fields. I worked as a housekeeper and in the market. My friends and I sew bags to sell.

I used to get drunk and get into fights but I got my salvation May 28, 2004. When I was little, I dreamed of being a nurse and of marrying a pastor. Now I serve as a Rural Health Motivator. I am trained in first aid to help my community. I am also a designated caregiver to look for signs of child abuse in my community and I report that to the police.

After I was saved, I couldn't notice what God wants and what God likes from me. I would just go on with my sins and just dragging them with me. I was thinking that I was following God.

When the West family came to Swaziland, I was just like, "Oh, what are these white people going to do to our lives, because we know Jesus." I didn't know that I was going the wrong, and Kay was like a friend to me at that time. I was like, "Oh, this lady is going to help me how?" I was dragging all these six children, I was going by sleeping with men without marriage, and I was like I was lost. I was just in the forest. And I didn't know that God doesn't want us to sleep without marriage.

I went closer to Kay and I expressed myself to her. That is why she sat down with me. She just cared for me with love and she didn't just scold me. I was just worried. I thought this lady [Kay]; she's not like the others I used to meet. She was just friendly to me. She came closer to me and she felt what I was feeling. I saw that she was in my boots at that time.

She [Kay] came closer to me and just asked me a question. That question I will never forget. "Is that what you are doing helping yourself or are you just using yourself?" I realized I was just using myself, and these men are going to just leave me with these babies, and I can't just live with them, and I can't just support these babies. I needed money to raise them up. I needed money for them to be educated because God says that they are a blessing to us. I have to manage them. I wish for the wisdom of Solomon to raise them.

So I was like, "Oh, what am I going to do with these children now?" Because I want to follow God. Kay came to me and she saw that I had a problem, and she asked, "What's your problem?" I just expressed my problem, "How, if I leave this man, who's going to support me? Who's going to give maybe that half a loaf of bread I was getting, who's going to give me that half a loaf of bread?" To me, she was like, "Okay, let's pray."

So we made a Moms in Prayer International group and there we will pray for our children, pray for our needs. And in time, God answered our prayers, especially for my prayer. It was just at that time answered.

And I got God's answers, and I have a home through the Wests, and my children are being supported now. The Wests came closer to me and they assisted in everything. I can express my house as a mansion. I can't even express it as a house because it's just big—three rooms with a veranda. It's just a mansion. When I come out from this home, they ask, "Who is the woman for this house? She's not worthy of this house." And you know, the community is just looking at me, and I'll tell them that it's only God that answers prayers perfectly. No one else.

And the men will come to me and propose love for me. I'll tell them that, "Oh no, I've got a good Husband, a faithful One, and He won't let me go. Every time He's with me. He's honest to me." And these men will say, "Oh, you're stupid." And I say, "OK, I'm stupid because the Word of God is stupid to those who are lost. But it is wise to those who have Christ." That's how they [John and Kay] helped me.

This family came like they were angels from God. That's what I can say about the Wests. And now they are away. Sometimes I miss them. And sometimes the devil will come, "Oh, you see, they are away now. How are you going to live?" I will say to him like Jesus told the devil when He had suffered for forty days. He said, "Man cannot live by bread only but by the Word of God." I tell the devil that I can live through God. Not through the wealth. Because God says that.

But I miss them. But in spirit I am with them. They are with me in spirit. They pray for me every day. And you know I succeed through many problems. Without God I can't live. I can say more but I am out of time now. Thank You, Jesus. Amen.

Kay Cassidy West

He Lifted Me Up from The Miry Clay (old Gospel song)

He lifted me up
from the deep miry clay.
He planted my feet
on the King's highway.
And this is the reason why
I sing and I shout,
My Jesus came down, down, down
And lifted me out.

Now to Him who is able to do exceedingly abundantly above all that we ask or think, according to the power that works in us, to Him be the glory in the church and in Christ Jesus to all generations, forever and ever. Amen. Eph. 3:20-21

Kay in her favorite place

Ncamsile, Ncamsile's son Thabiso, and Kay

Refiner's Fire

Kay doing a Moms in Prayer International training

Kay with the "All I know is that I love Jesus and that Jesus loves me" granny

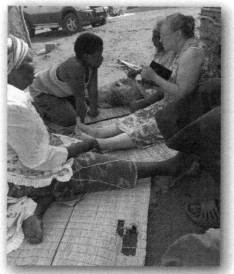
Kay leading a Bible study group

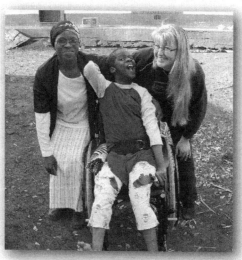
Jane, "Sister," and Kay

Kay with some of "her" ladies

Ncamsile and Kay

John, Kay, and Jeremy West.

Kay saying goodbye.

About the Author

Kay Cassidy West and her husband, John, were called as first-time missionaries to Swaziland, Africa when she was 47 years old and he was 49. They left behind successful careers and their older son, Zachariah. Kay has a master's degree in counseling and an associate's degree in ministry, and worked as a pastoral counselor as well as a private music teacher. Prior to God's call to the mission field, she had been active as a leader in women's ministry, a member of her church's worship team, a volunteer at a home for pregnant teens, and a leader at the local level for Moms in Prayer International (MIPI). None of that really matters. God called, so John and Kay, along with their younger son, Jeremiah, sold virtually everything to follow Him across the world.

Made in the USA
Lexington, KY
02 December 2016